THE COMPLETE GUIDE TO
OUR WORLD

STEVE PARKER

Sandy Creek
NEW YORK

CONTENTS

Words in **bold** are explained in the Glossary on page 138.

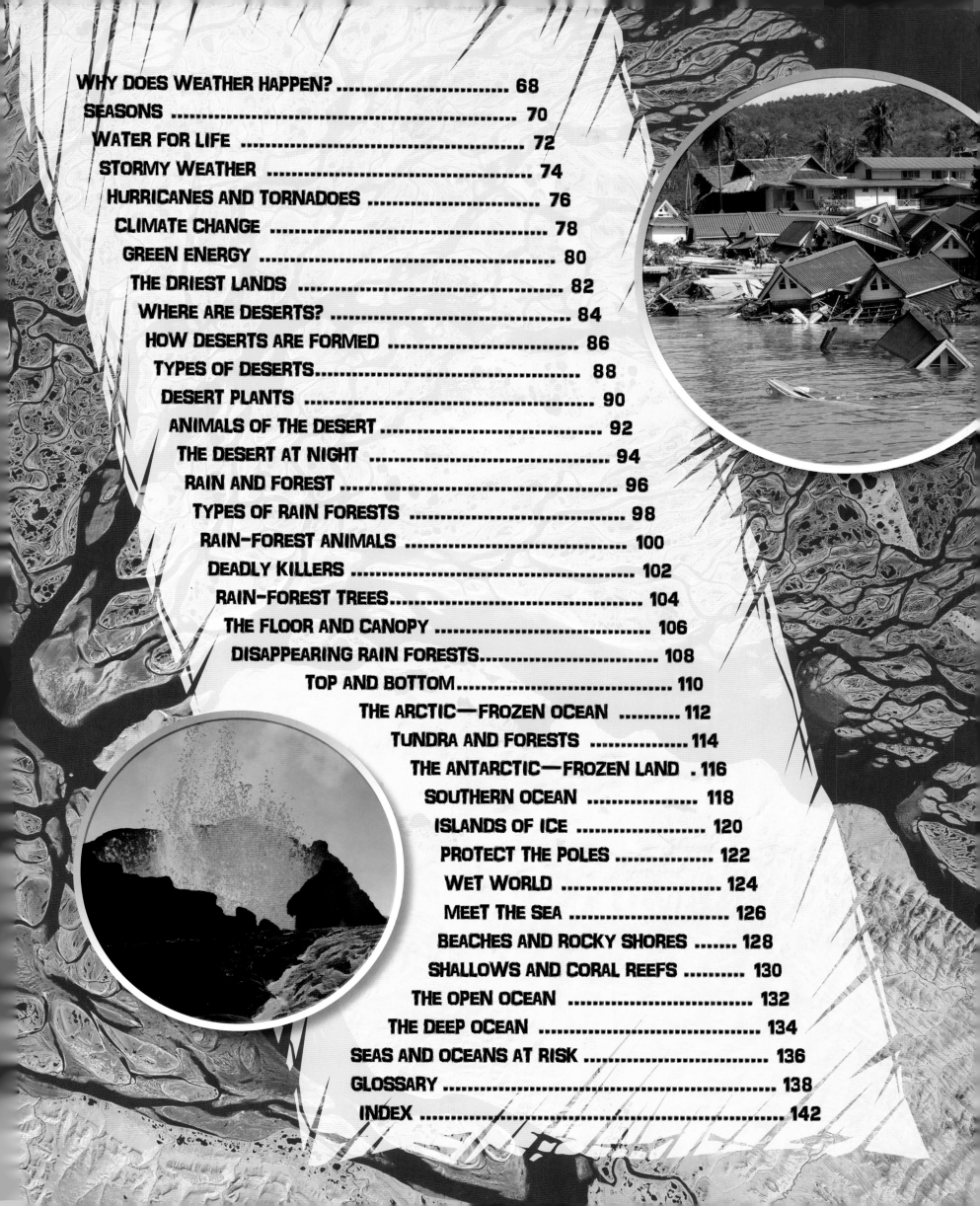

IN THE BEGINNING

To know what is inside Earth, we need to look back at where our planet came from. Its story started 4.6 billion years ago.

When a supernova takes place, it creates an enormous cloud of gas and dust.

Gas cloud

The star we call the Sun and all the objects going around it are together called the solar system. These objects include Earth and seven other planets, their moons, and countless smaller lumps of rock. They all began as a vast cloud of gas and dust spinning in space.

Sun and planets

As the cloud whirled around, small amounts of gas and dust began to clump together. This happened because of the pulling power that all matter has, called **gravity**. Some clumps slowly became bigger and heavier. The largest, in the center, formed the Sun and started to shine. Smaller clumps became the planets.

The Sun and planets gradually formed from a giant whirling cloud in space.

Earth is the fifth biggest of the eight planets and the third planet from the Sun in our solar system.

Mercury

Jupiter

Earth

Saturn

Mars

Neptune

Uranus

EARLY EARTH

As gas and dust clumped together to form Earth, they became extremely hot. Gradually, our planet took shape as a spinning ball.

Massive bang

Early in its history, it is possible that Earth was hit by another, smaller planet. This collision may have knocked a chunk out of Earth, and this became the Moon. The collision may also have tilted Earth, which does not spin upright, but slightly to one side.

A smaller planet may have crashed into Earth not long after it formed

EARTH FACT

The gas and dust cloud that formed our solar system was not the only one in space. Billions more formed other solar systems.

Red-hot world

Slowly, parts of Earth's surface began to harden into solid rock. Other parts of the surface remained as red-hot liquid rock. Huge volcanoes spurted out poisonous gases in many places. There was no life for a billion years.

The surface of the early Earth was made up of boiling rocks and huge volcanoes.

Bringing water

During our solar system's early history, there were millions of lumps of rock and ice hurtling around in space. Thousands of these smashed into Earth. Some of them, called **comets**, may have brought water to Earth as it cooled.

This is just one of many other solar systems in space; some are even being formed right now!

LAYERED EARTH

Earth is made up of layers. These start with the inner core at the center, and end with the **crust**.

Where rocks have been worn away, we can see deeper into the crust.

Earth's crust

The outer layer of Earth is known as the crust. In some places, such as the bottom of the sea, the crust is only 3 miles thick. In other places, especially under mountains, it can be up to 37 miles thick. The crust is not one solid piece. It is made of huge pieces with jagged edges, a little like a gigantic jigsaw puzzle.

Earth's crust is broken into eight large plates and many smaller ones.

Hot mantle

Under the crust is a much thicker layer called the **mantle**. This is about 1,800 miles deep. The rocks here are very hot and partly molten, or melted. They move and flow like thick jelly. The crust's pieces slide around slowly on the mantle.

Miners in South Africa travel deep under Earth's surface to find gold.

Inner core

At the center of Earth is the core. This is made up of the metals iron and nickel. Although the outer core is molten, the inner core is solid and very hot.

Earth's four main layers are the crust, the mantle, the core, and the inner core.

Mantle

Crust

Outer core

THE MANTLE

The mantle forms more than four-fifths of the entire Earth. It is so hot that some of its rocks are molten.

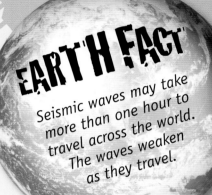

Moving mantle

The outer part of the mantle, at the bottom of the crust, has a temperature of about 930 degrees Fahrenheit. The inner mantle, next to the core, is more than 7,000 degrees Fahrenheit. Rocks in the mantle slowly flow up, sideways, and down again.

Shock waves from an earthquake show up as wavy lines on a machine called a seismograph.

Shock waves

An earthquake is the sudden jolting of the enormous **tectonic plates** of Earth's crust as they rub past each other. This jolting sends out shock waves, also called seismic waves. Some waves travel through the crust. Others pass into Earth and are bent by the mantle and core to reach Earth's surface far away. The speed and extent of bending show us what the mantle is made of.

Seismic waves bend as they pass through Earth's mantle and core.

Crust

Mantle

Outer core

Inner core

Earthquake

During an earthquake, the ground can shake and move so much that buildings collapse. This happened in Haiti in 2010.

ROCKY CRUST

The rocks that form our planet are made in different ways. This gives them different properties.

Soft rocks have been worn away by wind and rain to leave these hard granite rocks.

Rock types

There are three basic rock types. These are **igneous**, **sedimentary**, and **metamorphic rocks**. Igneous rocks form when extremely hot and runny **lava** or **magma** cool down and become solid.

Magma rocks

The molten rock deep in Earth's crust and mantle is called magma. This runny rock can rise up closer to the surface, cool, and then harden into an igneous rock, such as granite. These rocks are seen when the surface of Earth is worn away by wind and rain to uncover deeper layers.

Red-hot lava oozes slowly from some volcanoes and spurts out with a fiery explosion from others.

This lava has cooled into long, sausagelike shapes known as pahoehoe, or ropy lava.

Lava rocks

Magma can also rise up to the surface through a weak part in Earth's crust. When this happens in volcanoes, the magma is called lava. The lava flows out, cools, and hardens into igneous rocks of different shapes and patterns.

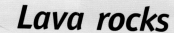

LAYERS OF ROCK

Sedimentary rocks are made from millions and millions of tiny pieces, or particles, of rocks that have been squeezed together.

Squashed into rock

Over millions of years, wind, rain, rivers, and ice wear away parts of Earth into tiny pieces, such as sand, mud, and **silt**. These get washed into rivers and are carried out to sea, where they sink to the bottom in layers known as **sediment**. As the layers pile up, the lowest ones are squashed into rocks, such as sandstone and limestone.

Layers of particles on the seabed are pressed into sedimentary rocks.

Sedimentary layers on the seabed

Earth's movements break the layers

The Painted Hills in Oregon, were once silt, clay, and mud left when a river flooded the land.

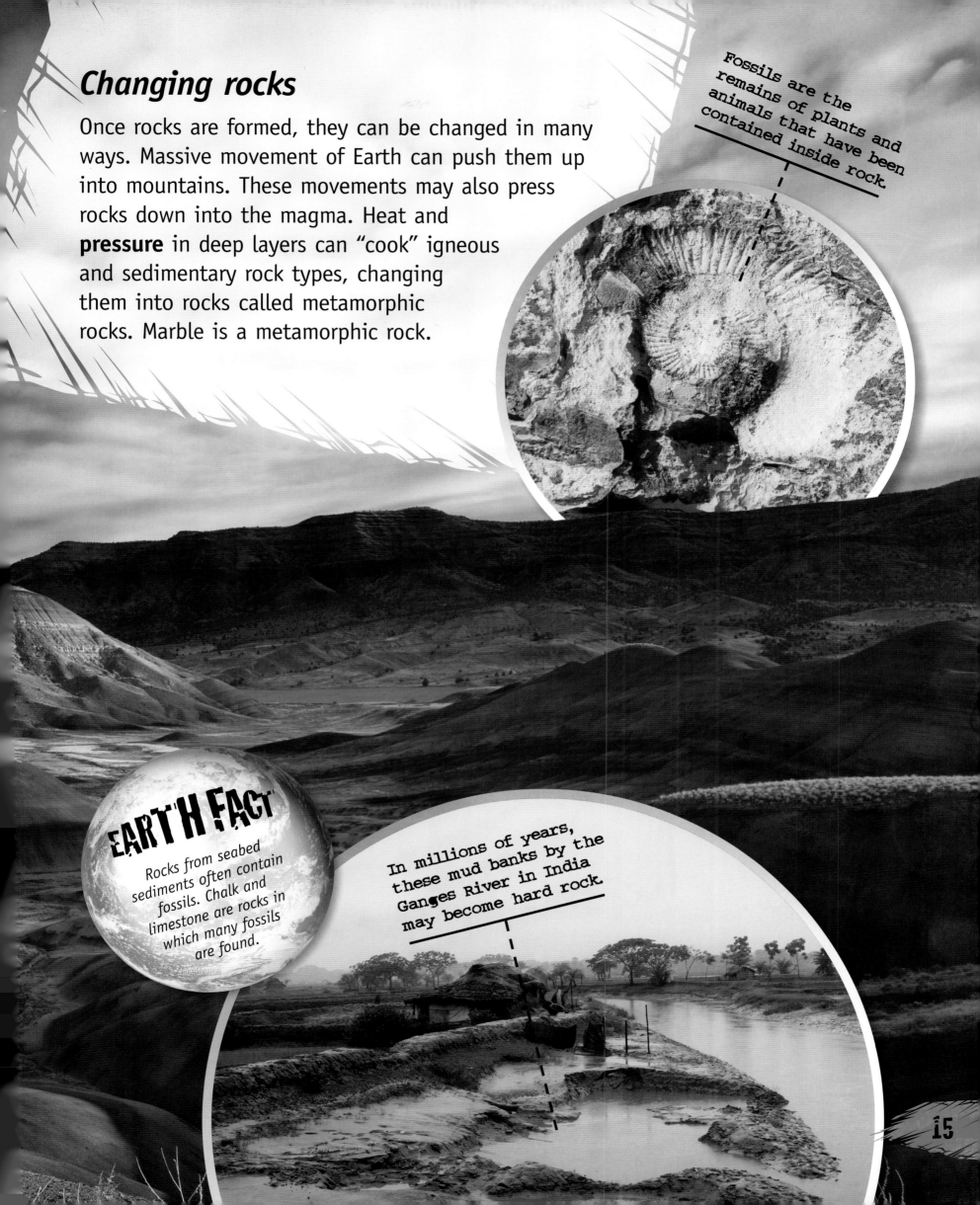

Changing rocks

Once rocks are formed, they can be changed in many ways. Massive movement of Earth can push them up into mountains. These movements may also press rocks down into the magma. Heat and **pressure** in deep layers can "cook" igneous and sedimentary rock types, changing them into rocks called metamorphic rocks. Marble is a metamorphic rock.

Fossils are the remains of plants and animals that have been contained inside rock.

EARTH FACT

Rocks from seabed sediments often contain fossils. Chalk and limestone are rocks in which many fossils are found.

In millions of years, these mud banks by the Ganges River in India may become hard rock.

15

CAVES

Rainwater that seeps deep into the cracks in rocks sometimes creates amazing cave systems.

Cracks and shafts

After it rains, water seeps into the ground through the soil. This rainwater will gradually sink deeper and deeper through cracks in the rock. Sometimes, streams and even small rivers can disappear through a vertical shaft called a **sinkhole**. The water may reappear again many miles away.

Streams eat tunnels and caves into limestone hills.

Stream disappears

Cave

Sinkhole

Spring

Stalactites form very slowly, drip by drip. They sometimes get so heavy, they break off.

Limestone caves

Most caves form in limestone rock. This is because limestone is slowly **dissolved**, or eaten away, by rainwater. At first the caves are full of water. As more limestone dissolves, the caves deepen and the higher parts become dry. Water that drips from the roof leaves behind particles of limestone that form icicle-shaped stalactites. Where it drips onto the floor, it can build upside-down versions known as stalagmites.

Stalagmites "grow" about 0.8 inches every 100 years.

17

EARTH MINERALS

Rocks are made of substances called **minerals**. Some of these are very precious and beautiful.

Rare and precious

Minerals form deep inside Earth over long periods of time. Some, such as gypsum, calcite, and various kinds of salt, are very common. Others, such as diamonds and gold, are rare and precious. Some rocks are also valuable. These include granite and marble, which are used in buildings.

Mexico's Cave of Crystals contains amazing crystals, some are even more than 30 feet long.

Pure gold is sometimes found within streams.

18

Digging mines

To take rocks and minerals from Earth, we dig mines. In a deep-shaft mine, sideways tunnels are made at the bottom of a deep hole. Open-pit, or opencast mines and quarries, or giant pits, are created near the surface. Rocks and minerals are removed from these using huge excavator machines and explosives.

This dynamite is being broken apart by explosives.

EARTH FACT

Diamonds are made deep inside Earth. They are carried to the surface by the flow of magma from Earth's core.

Amethyst is a form of the mineral quartz

19

FOSSILS

When animals and plants die, their bodies usually rot away. After a few years, there is nothing left. In some cases, however, **traces** of the hard parts of their bodies remain.

How fossils form

Fossils are found in sedimentary rocks. They are both the preserved hard parts of animals, such as bones, teeth, and shells, and the impression, or shape, of animals left in the mud. Many fossils of the hard parts of plants, such as the bark and seeds, have also been found. The parts are buried in sediments, and, like those sediments, they gradually turn into solid rock over millions of years.

EARTH FACT

In 2009, fossil hunters found the world's biggest dinosaur footprints in France. Each was about 5 feet across!

Fossils enable scientists to reconstruct the skeletons of ancient creatures.

Fossil record

Fossils tell us about the kinds of animals and plants that lived in the past. This is called the fossil record. It shows how life evolved, or changed, over millions of years. Knowing how fast the layers of sedimentary rocks were laid down allows scientists to figure out the age of the fossils.

Curly shelled ammonites are common fossils.

These fossil bones have been put back together to make the skeletons of a huge plant-eating dinosaur and two smaller meat eaters.

WHAT SHAPES EARTH?

Earth's surface is changing all of the time. Strong winds, heavy rain, freezing ice, fierce storms and rushing floods alter the land. Our coasts are changed by waves, ocean **currents** and unstoppable tides.

Ice and water

Freezing and melting ice can crack rocks. Huge **glaciers** of ice carve deep valleys, and rivers move rocks and soil from one place to another.

Volcanoes erupt and build new peaks, such as in the Tengger mountains in Java, Indonesia.

EARTH FACT

During sandstorms, sand may be blown away from one place, leaving behind bare rocks. The sand may fill a valley elsewhere.

Mighty forces

Many changes that shape Earth are very slow. But others are sudden and violent, such as powerful earthquakes and erupting volcanoes.

Human impact

People are altering Earth in many ways. We build cities with tall buildings, cut down forests, and change the way rivers flow. We drain **wetlands** and push back the sea to make fields for **crops**. Today, huge areas of land are being shaped by us.

New York City stands on land that was once thick with forests.

Deserts were once places filled with water and plants.

23

BUILDING UP

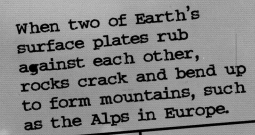

EARTH FACT

The fossils of sea creatures are found on mountains! This is because mountains were once part of the seabed.

Huge mountains have risen up in many parts of the world. Most of these mountains formed over millions of years, but, incredibly, some islands have formed in just one day.

Earth's plates

Earth's hard outer layer of rock, called the crust, is not one solid shell of rock. It is more like a cracked egg that is made up of giant, curved plates of rock. These jagged plates move slowly over millions of years. When two plates push together, their edges bend and crumple to form tall, sharp-topped mountains.

When two of Earth's surface plates rub against each other, rocks crack and bend up to form mountains, such as the Alps in Europe.

When two of Earth's plates move apart, they leave a huge crack in the surface, such as the Great Rift Valley in East Africa.

Exploding volcanoes

In some places, Earth's rocky crust is much thinner than in others. Red-hot liquid rock called lava lies just below this thin crust. This liquid rock may build up so much pressure that it pushes through the crust to form a volcano. The lava can ooze out or burst out as an **eruption**.

Hot liquid rock from volcanoes cools at the surface and hardens.

Fossils of sea creatures, such as this one, have been found high up on mountains.

25

WEARING DOWN

Earth's surface is shaped by the forces of wind, rain, frost, and ice. These slowly wear away the land in a process called **erosion**.

Erosion underground

Rainwater trickles down through cracks in rocks, slowly working its way deeper and deeper. The steady trickle dissolves some rock, such as limestone, making small cracks larger. This type of erosion eats away rocks under the surface to form huge caves and caverns—some are even as large as cities!

The Mammoth Caves in Kentucky were made by rainwater erosion.

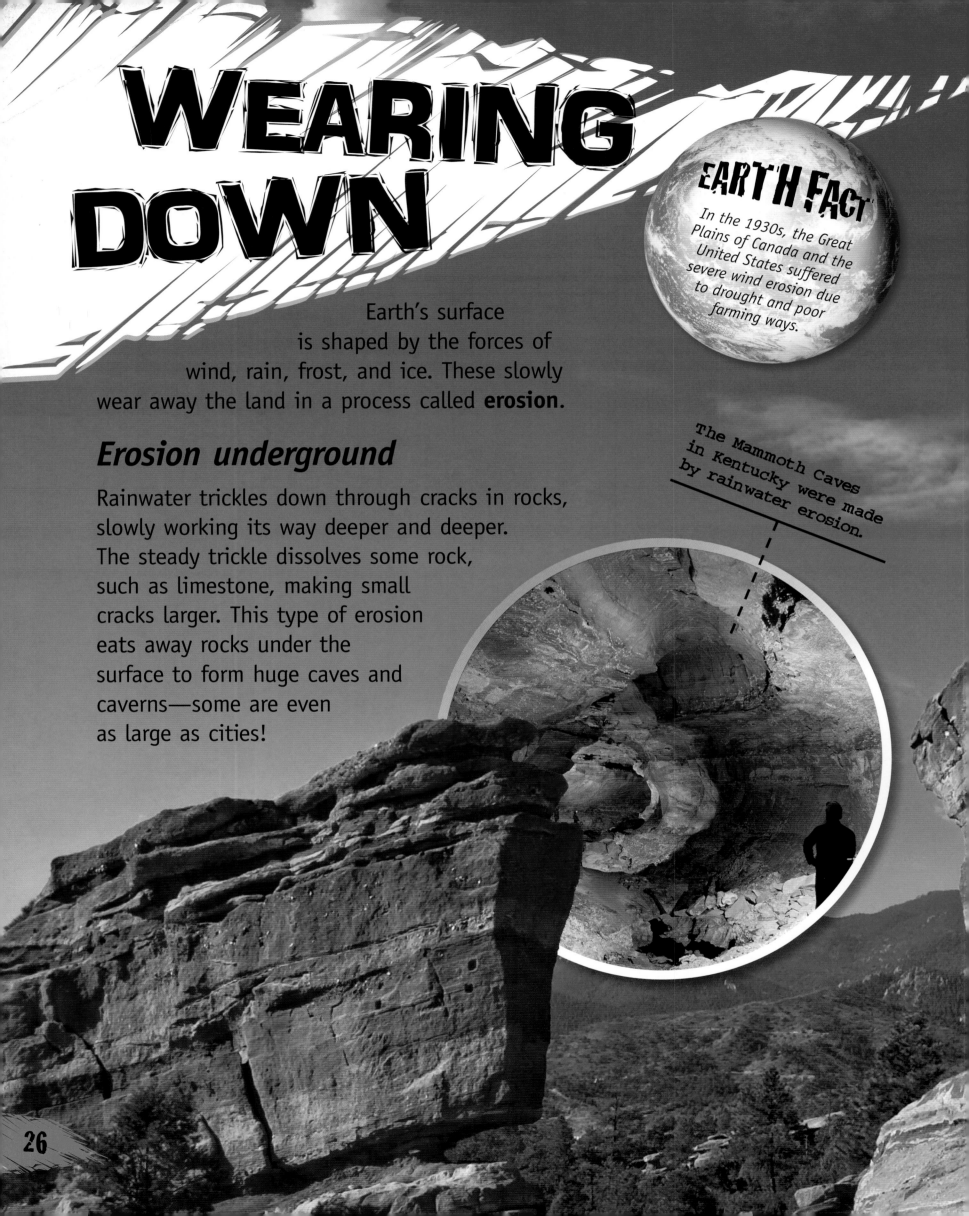

26

Power of ice

When water trickles into cracks in rocks and freezes into ice, it expands, or spreads out. This **expansion** forces open the cracks, making them wider. Slowly, over months and even years, pieces of rock break off and split into smaller rocks. This type of water erosion happens underground as well as on Earth's surface.

Wind has sandblasted and eroded these rocks near Colorado Springs, Colorado.

This broken rock has been split by water freezing into ice.

Erosion by wind

A gentle breeze can pick up dust and blow it against rocks. Over thousands of years, this dusty breeze can wear away even the hardest rock. Strong winds hurl around larger pieces, such as sand and gravel, which can erode rocks into strange shapes.

RIVERS

Rivers flow from high to low ground. On their journey, they erode hills and mountains, sometimes cutting deep **gorges**. Rivers also carry water to dry places, allowing plants to grow.

Rivers are powerful enough to cut deep mountain gorges.

At just over 4,160 miles, the enormous Nile River in Egypt is the longest river in the world.

In the mountains

Rivers start out in hills and mountains. Water flows down slopes in small streams, which join together to form larger streams and then rivers. As a river gets near the coast, it crosses areas of flatter land and flows more slowly. Sand, mud, and other bits settle along its bed and banks. Heavy rain can flood these flat areas, which are known as **floodplains**.

Out to sea

When the river reaches the sea, it deposits more material. Often, the river spreads out into many channels, forming a **delta**. After this, any material that is still carried by the water flows out to the sea.

Lack of water

If not enough rain falls, rivers can dry up and even disappear. If people take out too much water, such as for industry or farming, rivers may also turn into dry, cracked channels.

River deltas are made up of many smaller channels.

The Grand Canyon in the U.S.A. was formed over many millions of years by the Colorado River.

EARTH FACT

In parts, the Grand Canyon is almost 6,000 feet deep!

29

ICE RIVERS

During the last **ice age**, much of Earth was covered by ice sheets and glaciers. Today, glaciers are found only in the very coldest regions on Earth.

Changing landscape

About 20,000 years ago, during the last ice age, parts of North America and Northern Europe were covered with ice. This ice began to melt 10,000 years ago when the world warmed up. Although much of the ice is gone today, we can still see how it changed the landscape.

North America

Northern Europe

The white areas show the extent of ice 20,000 years ago.

Floating ice is a danger to boats in Glacier Bay, Alaska.

Huge valleys

The biggest changes to the landscape were made by massive "rivers" of ice called glaciers. These formed high up mountains, where it was too cold for snow to melt. Falling snow piled up, pressing on snow beneath to form hard-packed ice. This ice then moved slowly down the mountain, carving out a huge valley. Today, glaciers are found only in the highest mountains and in the **polar regions**, where it is freezing all year.

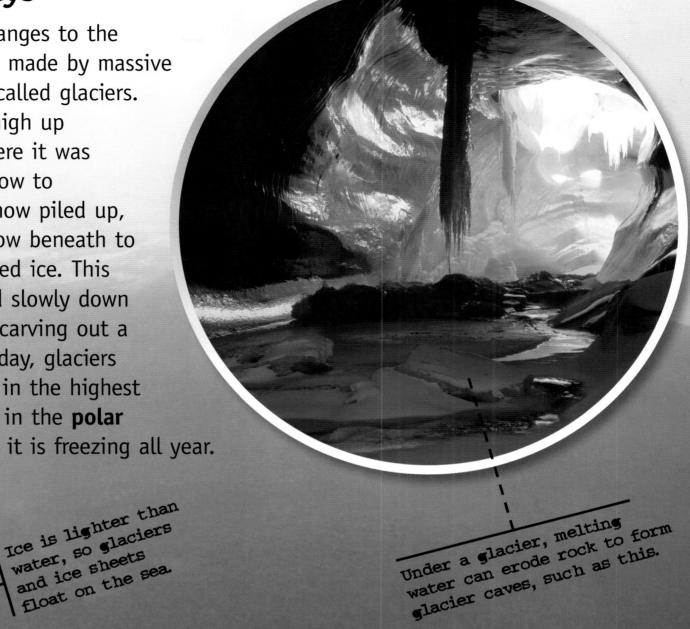

Ice is lighter than water, so glaciers and ice sheets float on the sea.

Under a glacier, melting water can erode rock to form glacier caves, such as this.

Massive icebergs

Most glaciers melt as they slide down mountains to where it is warmer. Some glaciers, however, are still frozen when they reach the sea. Huge chunks of ice can break off these glaciers and float away as icebergs.

EARTH FACT

Some of our glaciers are melting very quickly. If too much ice melts into the ocean, it could cause flooding in some places.

GLACIER POWER

Glaciers carve out deep valleys and move large amounts of rock and other material from one place to another. These features can be seen where the glaciers have long since disappeared.

Lysefjord in southern Norway is around 25 miles long.

This U-shaped valley was carved out by a glacier.

EARTH FACT

Glacier ice is made from snow that fell long ago. It may contain windblown seeds and even tiny animals.

Flooded valleys

When a valley that has been made by glaciers runs into the sea, it may be flooded by seawater. This type of flooded river valley is known as a **fjord**. Many fjords are found in some northern European countries, particularly along the coast of Norway. During the last ice age, Norway was entirely covered in ice.

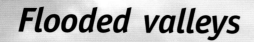

We study glaciers to find out what Earth was like long ago.

Rising land

During the last ice age, the huge weight of ice pushed down the land. As the **climate** became warmer and the ice melted, the ground started to move up again. This movement is still happening today. In Glacier Bay, Alaska, so many large glaciers have melted over thousands of years that the land still rises by 3 inches a year.

Alaska's Glacier Bay was underwater 20 years ago.

COASTAL AREAS

By day and night, Earth's coasts and shores are battered by the sea. Strong seawalls can help protect some coastal areas from the worst effects of this coastal erosion.

Sea attack

As waves crash into the bottom of a cliff, they smash its hard rock to pieces. Gradually, the waves eat away the cliff base, and the top of the cliff collapses into the sea. Any buildings on the cliff fall into the sea, too.

Harbor walls protect boats from big waves. They also provide people with a solid place from which to fish!

One of these cliff-top buildings is already sliding down to the sea.

New land

Along the coast, waves and currents roll and break big rocks into smaller pieces, such as shingle, sand, and mud. These are carried by tides and currents along the coast to make sandy beaches, sand dunes, and mud flats. Over a long period of time, these areas build up into new land.

This land in Eemnes, the Netherlands, has been reclaimed by digging channels to drain away water.

These concrete blocks and the reinforced wall protect the coastline.

TIDAL TIMES

A tide is the daily rise and fall of water in a sea or in an ocean. As it goes up and down, water wears away seaside sand and rocks and slowly shapes the shoreline.

At low tide, the waves have gone and there is no erosion.

High and low

The Moon's gravity makes the ocean closest to it bulge toward it. We call this high tide. At the same time, there is another bulge of water on the opposite side of Earth. Between these two high tides, there is a low tide. As Earth spins around each day, these bulges move around its surface.

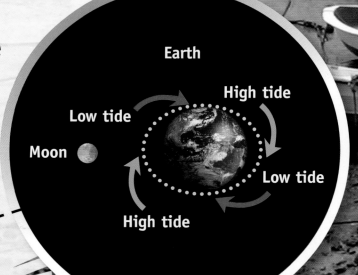

Earth

High tide

Low tide

Moon

Low tide

High tide

The yellow dots show how the Moon's gravity cause the oceans to bulge.

Worn by the tides

As tides rise and fall, they make seawater rush through narrow places, such as between the mainland and nearby islands. The rushing water adds power to the waves and the ocean currents. This causes mud, sand, and pebbles to scrape along the coast and reshape the shore.

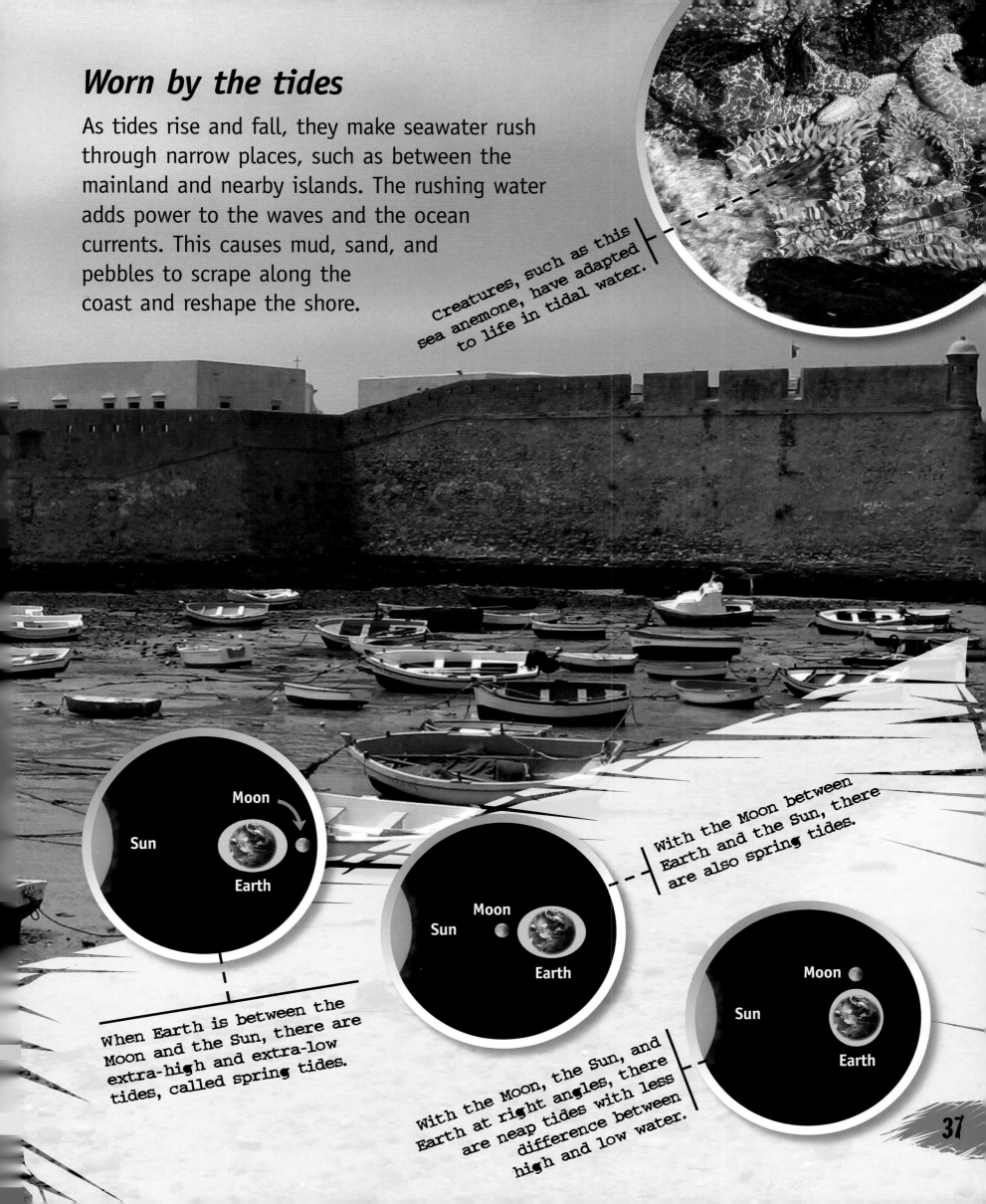

Creatures, such as this sea anemone, have adapted to life in tidal water.

With the Moon between Earth and the Sun, there are also spring tides.

Sun **Moon** **Earth**

When Earth is between the Moon and the Sun, there are extra-high and extra-low tides, called spring tides.

Sun **Moon** **Earth**

With the Moon, the Sun, and Earth at right angles, there are neap tides with less difference between high and low water.

Sun **Moon** **Earth**

SHAPING THE SEABED

On land, there are valleys, cliffs, mountains, and **plains**. Under the sea, there are similar features—but even bigger! These are shaped by many kinds of underwater forces.

In the shallows

Around Earth's **continents** are shallow parts of the ocean known as continental shelves. The water there is usually less than 490 feet deep, and the seabed is mostly flat. Some areas are covered by sand, silt, and mud that is carried from the land by rivers. In other places, the tides and currents wash away the sand, leaving bare rocks and stones on the seabed.

At the edge of the sunlit continental shelf, the seabed goes down into the cold, dark depths.

A sonar image of the continental shelf off the coast of California

Deep sea

Beyond the continental shelves are steep slopes and cliffs. These lead down to huge deep-sea plains that are covered with thick mud. In places, there are chains of mountains, narrow gorges, and volcanoes, similar to those found on land.

EARTH FACT

It is difficult to explore the deepest ocean because of the water's great pressing force, known as pressure.

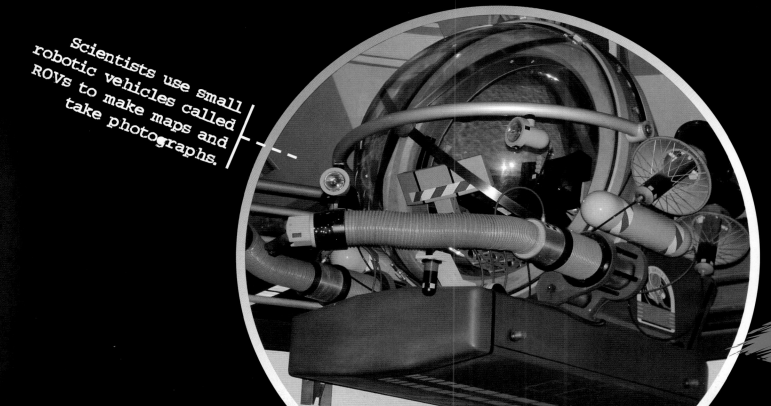

Scientists use small robotic vehicles called ROVs to make maps and take photographs.

WEATHER AND LIFE

The weather is different across Earth. Hot or cold, dry or wet, it enables plants and animals to live in some places and not in others. Both weather and living things help shape Earth.

Severe weather erodes high mountains such as these, making them lower and rounder.

Lifeless regions

The coldest places on Earth are the polar regions in the far north and south and the tops of mountains. There, it is too cold for living things to survive, and there are no plants to cover the land. The extreme weather on mountaintops, including rain, wind, snow, and ice, wears away the rocks. They break into pieces that roll down the slopes.

Along a tropical shore, mangrove trees protect the land from waves.

Protected by plants

In tropical places on Earth, it is almost always warm all year around. If there is also plenty of rain, living things grow quickly. Rain forests cover some parts of the land in the **tropics**, and mangrove trees grow along the shores. These huge, strong plants protect the soil and rocks from extreme weather, such as storms and floods.

Tree roots can force apart rocks and even make cliffs collapse.

Seasonal changes

Between the tropics and the poles, most places have a warm summer and a cool winter. During the summer, the Sun's heat makes cracks in rocks. In the cold winter, the rain and ice make the cracks wider. Over thousands of years, the rocks split apart. Whole mountains wear down, and the shape of the landscape changes.

When volcanoes erupt, they throw out huge amounts of hot rock, which reshapes the nearby landscape.

ANIMAL ACTION

Living things can have a big effect on the land's shape and its features, and everything plays its part. Even tiny bugs and worms can help break up rocks and change the flow of rivers.

Roots and leaves

Plant roots stop sand and soil from being blown away. This allows bigger plants to take root and grow in the soil. When fallen leaves gather on the ground, they rot to make the soil even richer and deeper.

Beavers changed the direction of this stream, which is now dry and rocky.

Watery homes

Beavers build huge dams across streams when they make their homes. These dams cause large areas of land around their home to flood, creating a lake. This water protects the beavers from **predators**, such as wolves. It also creates excellent wetland homes for many kinds of plants and animals.

This massive tree dam built by beavers has blocked the river.

EARTH FACT

If you joined all the tiny tunnels in 10 square feet end to end, they would stretch about a mile.

Rich soil contains hundreds of earthworms in every square foot.

Tiny workers

The small creatures that eat dead plants and animals, such as worms, slugs, and insects, change the land. Their tunnels allow air and water into the soil so that more plants can grow into woods and forests.

If animals, such as rabbits, were to eat the grass on these sand dunes, the grass might die out and the sand could blow away.

HOW WE CHANGE THE LAND

Long ago, people hardly changed Earth at all. Rather than farming, they hunted a few wild animals and gathered wild plants to eat. Today, the landscape is very different. Huge areas are covered with fields for farm animals and crops.

Some trees lose their leaves in the winter, which is good for the soil.

Farming the land

In the past, farms were built where trees and forests once grew. People cut down the trees and used the wood to make their farmhouses, their furniture, and other useful things. Then they planted grass on the land for cows, sheep, and other animals and grew crops, such as wheat, barley, and rice.

Losing forests

Changing land from forest to farmland can cause serious problems. This is because fields for crops and animals are not as good at soaking up heavy rain as forests are. During a heavy downpour, rainwater washes away the useful soil from fields. This soil, heavy with water, then clogs ditches and rivers.

Worn-out soil

Natural grasslands are much better than farmland at coping with a lack of water. During a long period without rain, called a drought, most farm crops die, as they need a lot of water to grow. This leaves the soil without plant roots to hold it together, and it can blow away as dust.

Floodwaters from farm fields can wash into towns and cities.

Natural rain forests can soak up very heavy rain without causing floods.

EARTH FACT

Poor farming is reshaping huge areas that were once wood and grasslands. It turns the land into dry, desertlike dust.

Keeping too many farm animals may make the soil dry and thin.

HUMAN IMPACT

When we build houses, stores, roads, and parks, wild places have to be cleared to make way for the building. Sometimes, this can have a damaging effect on wildlife and on the natural **environment** in which we live.

Roads and buildings

Earth is being shaped more and more by the people who live on it. New roads and buildings, for example, are using up more and more land. Sometimes, the way a river flows has to be changed to make way for a new town. This can cause the river to flood when there is heavy rain. Also, if people take out too much water from a river, it may dry up completely.

Every day, forests are cut down to make room for new towns.

Around the world, there has been a surge in road building.

Chemical pollution

We change Earth in ways that we cannot see. The chemicals we use every day can silently and invisibly pollute the air we breathe, the land in which we grow food, and even the water we drink. Increasingly, how people live, and the way in which we make the things that we use, is reshaping our world.

Heavy use of water has caused this river in China to dry up.

These windmills were built on reclaimed land.

MOVING WORLD

Earth's surface is continually moving. Some changes are very sudden, such as a volcanic eruption or an earthquake. Much bigger movements also happen, yet these are so slow that we hardly notice.

Changing world

Over millions of years, Earth's surface has changed many times. Rocks have been forced up to form mountains, which have then been worn away by wind and rain. Earthquakes have opened up huge cracks in Earth's surface, and hot volcanic material has covered vast areas of land.

New land is formed when molten rock from volanoes spews out onto Earth's surface.

Cracked surface

All of these changes happen because Earth is not solid rock. Inside, it is partially melted. On the outside, Earth is like a cracked egg, made of giant curved pieces called tectonic plates. The plates are pushed around by the swirling, partially melted rock beneath. These bump, rub, and crash together.

Venezuela's Angel Falls is the world's highest waterfall, with a height of 3,211 feet. It formed when a huge chunk of rock slipped.

All parts of a tectonic plate move, including the coastline. This area in Sognefjord, Norway, has moved 15.5 miles west in the last 10,000 years.

49

TECTONIC PLATES

Earth's crust, or outer layer, is made of jagged-edged tectonic plates. These are constantly on the move, drifting on the part-liquid rock beneath.

EARTH FACT

The San Andreas Fault is 808 miles long. In the last 150 years, it has caused four big earthquakes.

Building mountains

Under Earth's crust is the partially melted mantle. This swirls and flows very slowly, carrying the plates along with it. In some places, the plates push against each other and their edges crumple to form mountains and valleys.

Subduction zone, when one plate slides under another plate.

When two plates push against each other, they create mountains and valleys.

Sliding past

At a **transform fault**, two plates slide sideways past each other. This produces cracks in the ground and sometimes earthquakes. At the San Andreas Fault, which lies along the coast of western North America, the Pacific Plate slides past the North American Plate by more than 0.4 inches each year.

The San Andreas Fault is one of Earth's longest fault lines.

Mid-oceanic ridge, when two plates pull apart.

Transform fault is when two plates slide past each other.

There are seven major tectonic plates and many smaller ones.

Mid-ocean ridges

Mountain ranges, called mid-ocean ridges, are formed under oceans in places where two tectonic plates move apart. When hot magma is forced up through the gap, it hardens to form a ridge. The Mid-Atlantic Ridge is a mid-ocean ridge.

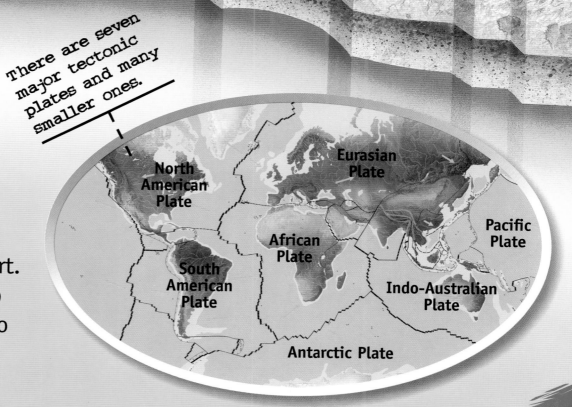

North American Plate

Eurasian Plate

African Plate

South American Plate

Pacific Plate

Indo-Australian Plate

Antarctic Plate

RING OF FIRE

All around the Pacific Plate are earthquake and volcano zones. These make up the "Ring of Fire".

Mapping the plates

Scientists know that where Earth's tectonic plates meet there are likely to be more earthquakes and volcanic eruptions. By keeping a careful record of all the earthquakes and eruptions that occur, scientists have been able to make a detailed map of Earth's tectonic plates.

China

Japan

North Pacific Ocean

Philippines

Indonesia

Australia

Schoolchildren in Japan know to get under their desks in the event of an earthquake.

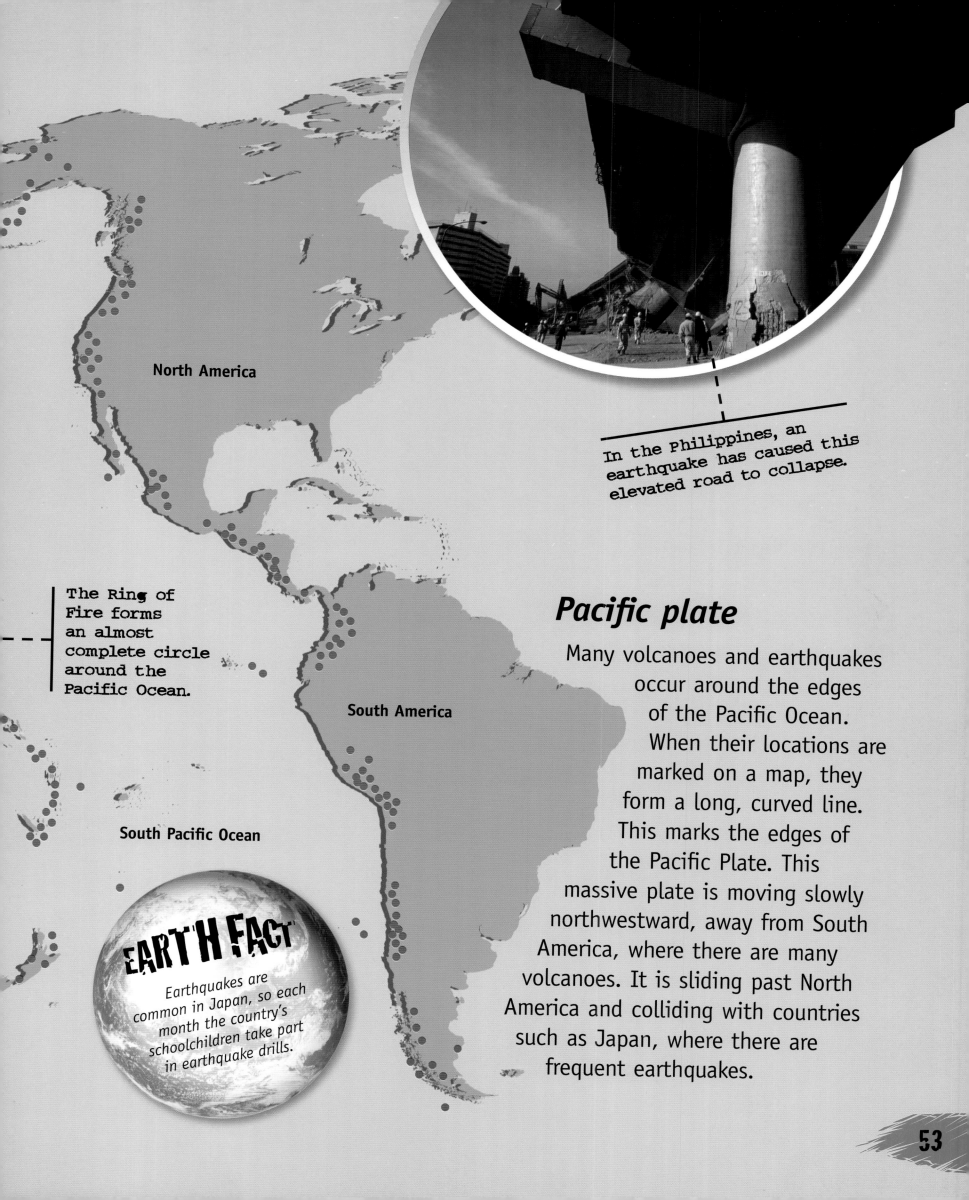

North America

The Ring of Fire forms an almost complete circle around the Pacific Ocean.

South America

South Pacific Ocean

Pacific plate

Many volcanoes and earthquakes occur around the edges of the Pacific Ocean. When their locations are marked on a map, they form a long, curved line. This marks the edges of the Pacific Plate. This massive plate is moving slowly northwestward, away from South America, where there are many volcanoes. It is sliding past North America and colliding with countries such as Japan, where there are frequent earthquakes.

EARTH FACT

Earthquakes are common in Japan, so each month the country's schoolchildren take part in earthquake drills.

MOUNTAINS

Mountains can be formed by volcanic activity as well as from movements in the tectonic plates.

Fold mountains

A type of mountain called a fold mountain is formed when tectonic plates squeeze against each other. When this happens, rock layers in Earth's crust are pushed up, which causes them to fold and then crack. New fold mountains usually have sharp, jagged peaks.

EARTH FACT

The highest place on Earth is the top of Mount Everest, which is 29,029 feet above sea level.

The Himalayas began to form about 70 million years ago. They are still rising.

Edinburgh Castle in Scotland was built on a volcanic plug.

Volcanic plugs

Mountains are also formed from the remains of volcanoes. These mountains, which are called **volcanic plugs**, are made when magma fills up a volcano's vent and hardens into rock. After millions of years, the outer part of the volcano may be worn away, leaving behind the plug.

The world's tallest mountain is Mauna Kea, an extinct volcano in Hawaii. Its height from seabed to summit is about 29,856 feet.

California's Half Dome Mountain was formed flat on one side.

Dome mountains

Sometimes, huge blocks of rock in Earth's crust are pushed up by the hot magma below. If the magma cannot find a way out through the crust, it may push up a weak part of the crust to form what is known as a dome mountain. This type of mountain, such as Half Dome Mountain in California, often has a flattened top.

WHAT IS A VOLCANO?

Volcanoes form when red-hot, runny rock pushes up from far below and out through Earth's crust.

Volcanic mountain

A volcano is a place in Earth's crust where material from deep inside forces its way out. Because this molten material is under great pressure, it can also form a mountain. The rock layers are pushed up by magma, or trapped melted rock. When the volcano erupts, lava and ash from the volcano can make the mountain bigger.

EARTH FACT

The soil around a volcano is often rich in minerals and good for growing crops.

As it flows, lava from an erupting volcano often looks like a red-hot river of rock.

Inside a volcano

Before a volcano erupts, magma rises through the mantle and collects in a large pool—called the magma chamber. When the pressure there is great enough, magma is forced up a pipe called the conduit. It then bursts out as liquid rock called lava.

Danger!

The biggest danger to people from a volcano is from huge, hot, poisonous clouds known as pyroclastic flows. These shoot out of the volcano and can travel downhill at 435 miles per hour. Anyone caught in a pyroclastic flow would be killed instantly.

The land around volcanoes is often used for farming because it is so rich.

Gas and ash cloud

Vent

Lava

Crater

Conduit (pipe)

Magma chamber

OTHER VOLCANOES

In some places, there are huge volcanoes called supervolcanoes. There are also many volcanoes under the sea!

Massive destruction

A supervolcano forms where magma cannot break through the crust. More and more pressure builds up over a wide area. Eventually, a huge area may explode with lava and ash. The effects would be felt all over the world and last for many years.

Scientists do not know when the next devastating supervolcanic eruption will take place.

EARTH FACT

The Lake Toba supervolcano in Sumatra, Indonesia, exploded about 75,000 years ago. It killed thousands.

Underwater rock shapes

Undersea volcanoes are like those on land. They occur along the edges of plates in the crust and erupt lava, ash, and gases. Lava cools quickly in seawater, forming strange rock shapes on the seabed.

Black smokers

When large pools of magma collect underground, cracks can appear in the crust. Very hot water spews out of these cracks. On land, these are known as **geysers**. Under the sea, they are known as black smokers.

NORTH AMERICA

Long Valley Caldera, California

Yellowstone, Wyoming

Valles Calderas, New Mexico

SOUTH AMERICA

EUROPE

AFRICA

ASIA

The Siberian Traps, Russia

Kyushu, southern Japan

Aira Caldera, Kagoshima

AUSTRALIA

Taupo Volcano, New Zealand

Scientists believe that there are seven sites worldwide that could become supervolcanoes in the future.

Undersea volcanoes pump out super-hot water via geysers.

59

EARTHQUAKES

Earthquakes can occur anywhere on Earth. The worst, however, usually strike parts of the world where the tectonic plates meet.

Violent movements

The worst earthquakes happen when the sideways pressure between two tectonic plates builds up so much that they move suddenly and violently. The center of an earthquake is usually deep underground. The place above it on the surface is called the **epicenter**.

4,600 people lost their lives in the 1995 earthquake that rocked Kobe, Japan.

Plates slip sideways

Epicenter

Shock waves spread out

Center

A sudden sideways movement of two tectonic plates can cause an earthquake.

In 1906, San Francisco, California, was hit by a huge earthquake.

EARTH FACT

Every day, there are about 3,000 earthquakes on Earth. Most are so small that no one notices them at all!

Plenty of warning

Many of the worst earthquakes have been unexpected. The city of San Francisco in California has been hit by several major earthquakes in the past. Today, scientists in this region measure what is happening deep underground in order to give people plenty of warning as to a possible earthquake.

LANDSLIDES

The landscape can change when parts of mountains or cliffs fall to the land or sea below. These are known as landslides or landslips.

Causes of landslides

Landslides can be caused by earthquakes, underground water during wet weather, or the wearing away of land to leave overhanging rocks. Landslides also happen when too many trees on hills and mountains are cut down. This can cause the entire side of a hill or mountain to slip down.

In 2002, an enormous 18-mile landslide in Koban Valley, Russia, killed 125 people.

Whole hillsides can slide away.

Deadly mudslides

When soil is very wet, it turns into mud. This is when a mudslide can strike. Mudslides, which can also carry many tons of rocks, may reach speeds of 50 miles per hour. Because mudslides are so unpredictable, they can be extremely dangerous.

Avalanches travel faster than people can run, or even ski

EARTH FACT

Landslides into the sea can cause **tsunamis**. When a huge amount of earth crashes into the sea, it can create a huge wave.

Danger to life

An avalanche is a mass of snow that rushes down a mountainside and can destroy buildings that lie in its path. Avalanches often start after heavy winter snow. They can be triggered by a simple human activity, such as snowboarding, or by natural events, such as high winds. In mountainous regions, avalanches pose the greatest danger to human life.

63

TSUNAMIS

A tsunami is a giant wave that rushes up from the sea and onto the land. This massive wall of water can destroy anything that lies in its path.

What causes tsunamis?

A tsunami may be triggered by a violent earthquake that pushes up the seabed. It can also be caused by an underwater volcano or even a huge landslide into the sea.

Even a small tsunami can wash away cars and break up roads.

Tsunamis travel many hundreds of miles before crashing onto shore.

Undersea earthquake

Low, fast surface waves

Wave builds higher

Wave slows down

Wave breaks onto shore

Wall of water

A tsunami usually starts deep in the ocean. At first, it looks like an ordinary wave on the ocean's surface. Ships far out at sea do not even notice it. At this point, the tsunami is moving very fast. As the sea becomes shallower around the coast, the tsunami slows and becomes higher.

The 2004 Indian Ocean tsunami killed more than 220,000 people.

Hitting the shore

Tsunamis can rise to the height of a two-story building just before they hit the shore. When a tsunami finally breaks, the force of the water is so strong that it destroys buildings and can move heavy objects far inland.

CLIMATE OR WEATHER?

Weather is what happens over hours and days. It can change very quickly. Climate, on the other hand, may not change for thousands of years.

This river in Saskatoon, Canada, regularly freezes during the winter.

Changing weather

Weather occurs over a short period of time—sometimes even just for a few minutes! In some places, it is easy to predict. In a tropical desert, for example, it is likely to be hot and dry, day after day. But in another place, the weather can be much more varied. Most summer days are warm, but any one day may be sunny or cloudy, wet or dry.

The Sun is shining, but the rainbow tells us that there is rain nearby.

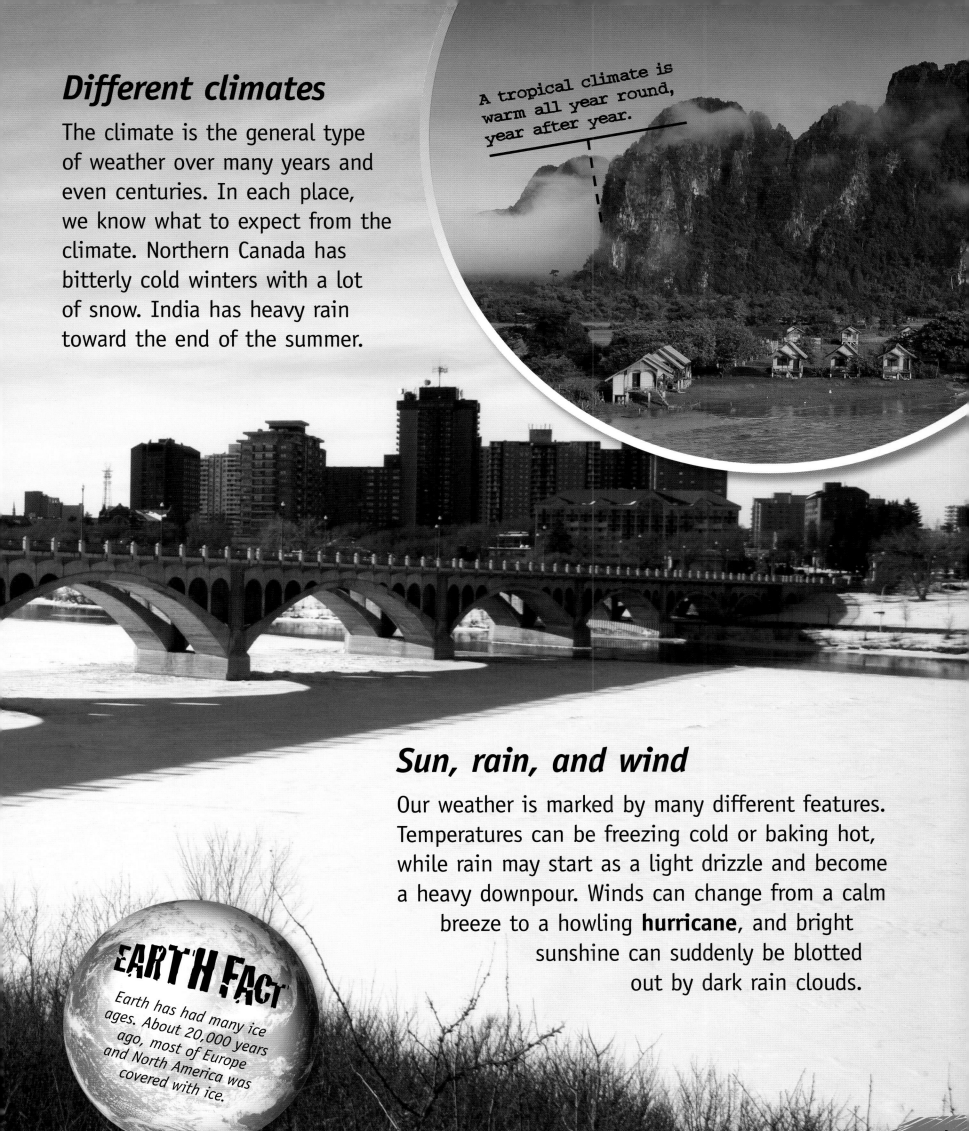

Different climates

The climate is the general type of weather over many years and even centuries. In each place, we know what to expect from the climate. Northern Canada has bitterly cold winters with a lot of snow. India has heavy rain toward the end of the summer.

A tropical climate is warm all year round, year after year.

Sun, rain, and wind

Our weather is marked by many different features. Temperatures can be freezing cold or baking hot, while rain may start as a light drizzle and become a heavy downpour. Winds can change from a calm breeze to a howling **hurricane**, and bright sunshine can suddenly be blotted out by dark rain clouds.

EARTH FACT

Earth has had many ice ages. About 20,000 years ago, most of Europe and North America was covered with ice.

WHY DOES WEATHER HAPPEN?

The heat of the Sun and the spinning of the planet are the most important factors that create our weather.

Our atmosphere

Earth's **atmosphere** is made up of a layer of gases. The atmosphere contains the **oxygen** that we breathe and protects us from the Sun's dangerous rays. As Earth turns, the Sun heats the air in the atmosphere by different amounts. As air gets warmer, it rises, and cooler air flows in to take its place. This current, or flow of air, creates winds. Winds can travel at different speeds and in different directions.

EARTH FACT

The hottest temperature ever recorded was 136.4 degrees Fahrenheit, in Libya, North Africa.

The Sun's warmth heats the middle of Earth more than the top and bottom.

Wind is the air of the atmosphere moving sideways from one place to another.

Hottest and coldest

The farther you go from the middle of Earth toward its top or bottom, the colder it becomes. The Sun heats the middle part of Earth the most, so it is always hot there. It also becomes colder the higher up above sea level you go. This height is called a place's **altitude**.

Even though Mount Kilimanjaro is close to the middle of Earth, its peak is at a high altitude, so it stays cold enough for snow.

SEASONS

Seasonal changes, which are caused by the Sun, affect many living things on Earth.

Four seasons

Between the poles and the tropics are the **temperate** lands. Most of these have four seasons—warm summer, cool fall, cold winter, and warming up again in the spring. In tropical places, it's warm all year, but there is usually a wet and a dry season.

Spring to life

All living things adapt to temperature changes and the amount of daylight that they get. Trees in temperate places are usually deciduous— they lose their leaves in the winter. There, also, animals may **hibernate** in the winter and seeds will not start to grow until the spring.

Spring

In the summer, the days are longer and warmer.

Fall

Why do we get seasons?

Earth is tilted as it moves around the Sun once each year. For part of the year, the northern half is closer to the Sun, giving summer there. For the other part of the year, Earth's southern half is closer and has its summer. Countries near the poles have just a few hours of winter daylight. On the **equator**, day and night are the same all year round.

EARTH FACT

Hammerfest, Norway has no sunlight from November 21 – January 21. Between May 17 – July 29, the Sun shines all day.

In the winter, the days are shorter and colder.

Summer in the Northern Hemisphere

Equator

Sun

Equator

Summer in the Southern Hemisphere

WATER FOR LIFE

Water is always moving around in a cycle between Earth and the sky. Nothing can live without water, but too much or too little can be harmful.

Cloud formation

The Sun's heat warms water in seas, lakes, and rivers. This causes **water vapor** to form. As the water vapor rises, it cools down and turns into millions of drops of water. These drops form clouds.

Heavy clouds gather over the land. There, in the distance, rain is falling.

72

Back to the ocean

When water drops in a cloud become too heavy, they fall as rain. If the air is very cold, they freeze and fall as snow. After falling, rain finds its way back to the ocean in rivers and the cycle begins once more.

Too much or too little

Droughts happen in places where rain usually falls each year. If the rains do not come, some crops and animals may die. When droughts last for several years, all plants die and the soil dries out and blows away. When too much rain falls over a period of time, the soil cannot soak it all up. Rivers may burst their banks and flood the land.

The spadefoot toad, which lives in the Sonoran Desert in North America, can stay in its burrow without eating or drinking for nine months!

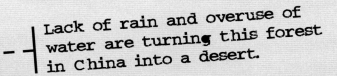

Lack of rain and overuse of water are turning this forest in China into a desert.

Clouds form in the cool air.

Water evaporates from the ocean.

Rain falls and water flows along streams and rivers back to the ocean.

STORMY WEATHER

A storm usually brings dark clouds, strong winds, rain, and sometimes thunder and lightning. These are caused by the Sun's heat quickly warming parts of the atmosphere.

Hot air rising from this desert has triggered a thunderstorm.

Wind and rain

Winds are made up of air that is moving from places where it has a higher pressure to areas of lower pressure. The greater difference there is in air pressure, the faster the wind moves. Winds faster than 55 miles per hour are called a storm. If warm, damp air meets cold air there, the water vapor turns to rain, which can be very heavy and cause floods.

Thunder and lightning

When raindrops rub against each other in a cloud, they create electricity. This electricity causes giant sparks to jump from one part of the cloud to another, or to shoot down to the ground. This is lightning. Lightning is extremely hot and heats up the air around it, which expands and forms giant **sound waves**. These waves make the booming sound that we call thunder.

This tree in the Ligurian Alps in Italy has been destroyed by lightning.

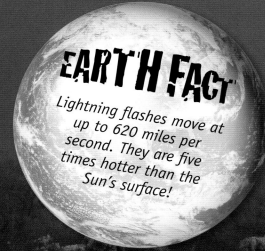

EARTH FACT

Lightning flashes move at up to 620 miles per second. They are five times hotter than the Sun's surface!

HURRICANES AND TORNADOES

A hurricane is a violent tropical storm that forms over warm waters close to the equator. **Tornadoes** are formed inside thunderclouds. They are spinning columns of air that cause great destruction.

Hurricanes

Hurricanes form in the heat of the summer. Water vapor rises from the ocean's surface, then when it reaches the top of the clouds, it cools and sinks, causing heavy rain. Air currents and the spinning of Earth then set the storm clouds spinning faster and faster.

A violent hurricane hits land in the tropics.

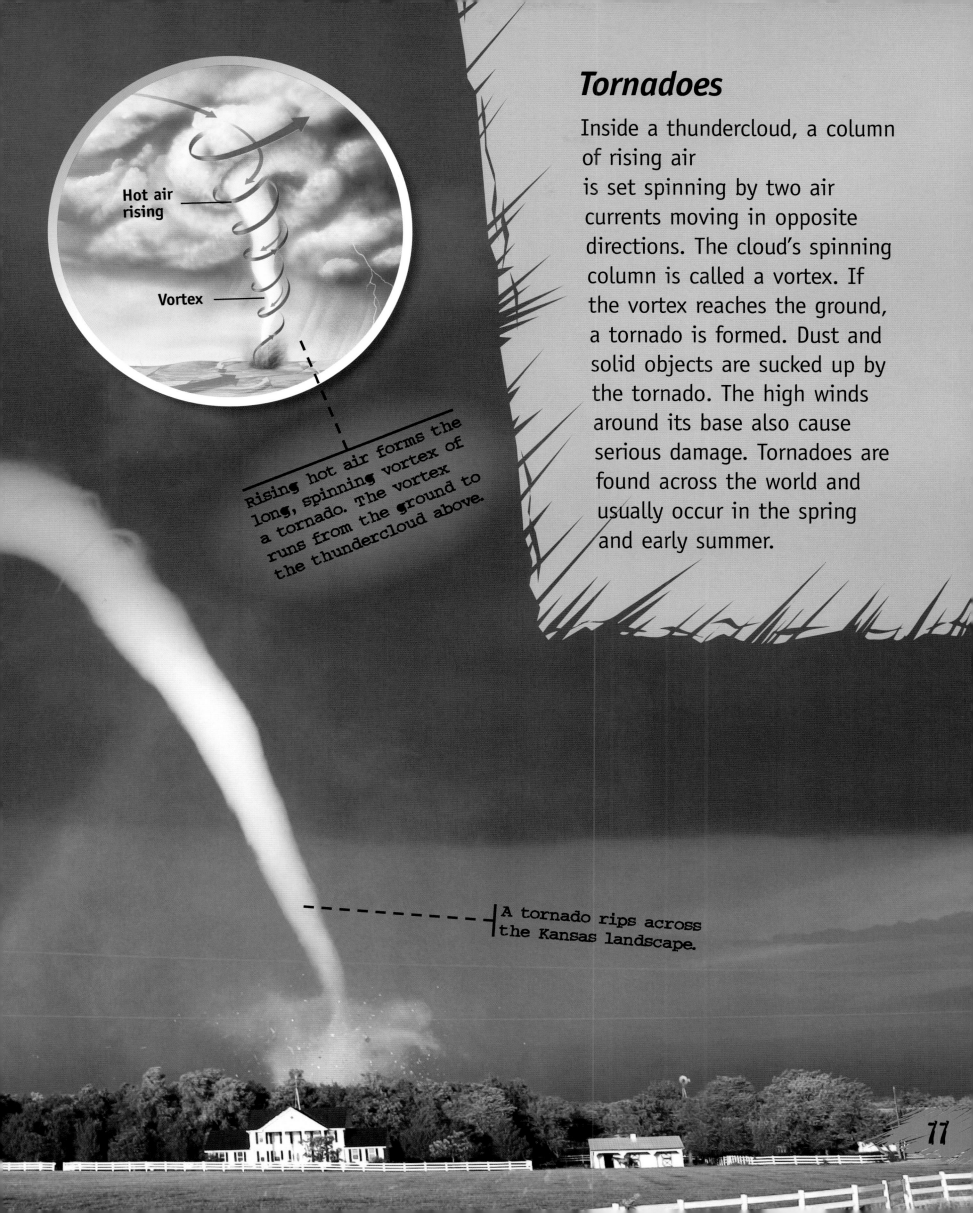

Tornadoes

Inside a thundercloud, a column of rising air is set spinning by two air currents moving in opposite directions. The cloud's spinning column is called a vortex. If the vortex reaches the ground, a tornado is formed. Dust and solid objects are sucked up by the tornado. The high winds around its base also cause serious damage. Tornadoes are found across the world and usually occur in the spring and early summer.

Hot air rising

Vortex

Rising hot air forms the long, spinning vortex of a tornado. The vortex runs from the ground to the thundercloud above.

A tornado rips across the Kansas landscape.

CLIMATE CHANGE

When we burn fuel in homes, vehicles, factories, and power plants, we make greenhouse gases that can cause climate change.

Constant change

Scientists believe that climate change is not new—Earth's climate has changed many times. When the dinosaurs walked on Earth, the world was much warmer than it is today. During the ice age, when much of Earth was covered with ice, it was much colder!

In some areas, climate change may mean that no rain falls, leading to drought.

Greenhouse gases stop warmth escaping from the atmosphere.

Less heat escapes into space

Atmosphere

Greenhouse gases trap more heat

Earth's surface

Floods and droughts

A warming world could have devastating consequences for many people. First, as the world's ice melts, sea levels will rise. This will flood low-lying land with salt water. There may also be more storms and droughts as the climate changes, making it difficult to live in some parts of the world.

In other areas, climate change may lead to heavy rain and floods.

The low-lying Maldive Islands in the Indian Ocean are threatened by rising seas.

GREEN ENERGY

To slow down the rate of climate change, we must use less energy. We also need to generate energy in ways that do not produce damaging carbon dioxide and other greenhouse gases.

Saving energy

Much of the energy that we use in our homes and factories is wasted. We can reduce this waste by using equipment that requires less electricity to work, such as low-energy lightbulbs. Another way we can save energy is to **insulate** buildings so that much less heat is lost through their walls and roofs.

Electricity-generating turbines at sea are sometimes grouped together as a wind farm.

EARTH FACT

Earth has energy, too! Engineers are finding ways to turn the power of waves and tides into electricity.

Wind power

Wind can be a problem—but it can be helpful, too! **Wind turbines** generate electricity without producing greenhouse gases. Many wind turbines are set up out at sea. It is more expensive to build these offshore, but the wind blows more steadily out at sea.

Solar energy

The Sun's energy, called solar energy, powers our weather and climate. We can turn sunlight into electricity by using devices called photovoltaic cells, which are mounted on solar panels. The Sun's warmth can also be used to heat water for homes and factories.

A solar power plant in Sanlucar, Spain.

THE DRIEST LANDS

Deserts can be sandy, rocky, or covered with pebbles. They can be scorching hot or freezing cold, but all deserts are very dry.

A large area of windswept sand in a desert is known as an erg.

People in the Gobi Desert live in tents called yurts and keep two-humped, Bactrian camels.

Dry and hot

All living things need water in order to survive but deserts do not have very much of it. This is because it hardly ever rains in a desert. If it does rain, the water usually dries in the hot Sun, trickles through the thin soil, or flows away over bare rock. This is why many deserts appear to have so little life.

Palm trees are one of the few plants that can survive in the desert.

The dorcas gazelle digs for plant bulbs in the desert.

Saving water

About one-quarter of the world's land area is either very dry or true desert. Yet even though these places are so **arid**, or dry, some plants and animals can survive there. These desert creatures and plants have special ways of saving what little water there is. Humans have lived in deserts for thousands of years, too. These people have adapted their way of life to suit it.

WHERE ARE DESERTS?

NORTH AMERICA

Great Basin

Mojave

Sonoran

Chihuahua

Sahara

Most of Earth's large deserts are found toward the middle of the world. They lie above and below the line called the equator.

Pacific Ocean

Atlantic Ocean

North of the equator

SOUTH AMERICA

Many of the world's largest deserts lie north of the equator. One reason for this is that there is more land to the north of the equator than there is to the south. The northern deserts include the Sonoran Desert in North America, the Sahara in North Africa, the Arabian Desert of the Middle East, and the Taklimakan and Gobi deserts in Asia.

Sechura

Atacama

Monte Patagonian

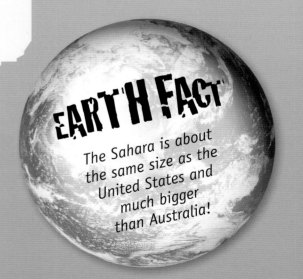

EARTH FACT

The Sahara is about the same size as the United States and much bigger than Australia!

84

Largest desert

The Sahara, which takes up 3,629,360 square miles, is the world's largest desert. It is about 3,100 miles across. This is almost the same distance as between London and New York!

EUROPE

Kara Kum

Gobi

Taklimakan

Turkestan

Thar

ASIA

Arabian

Somali

Indian Ocean

Equator

AFRICA

South of the equator

South of the equator, both Africa and South America have deserts. These are mainly in the southwest of each continent. North America has deserts in its southwest, too. The place with the most deserts compared to its size is Australia. More than two-thirds of this huge country is dry land or desert.

Kalahari

Namib

Great Sandy

Gibson   Simpson

Great Victoria

AUSTRALIA

In the middle of Australia, the desert stretches as far as you see.

The largest southern dry areas are in Australia.

Antarctic

HOW DESERTS ARE FORMED

Deserts form in places where there are few rain clouds. These can be inland, along dry coasts, and in areas shielded from rain by mountains.

Continental deserts

The way that Earth spins around and how it is warmed by the Sun affects how clouds form and where winds blow. Often, there are clouds and rain near sea coasts. Farther inland, it is drier. The largest deserts, such as the Sahara, Gobi, and Australian deserts, are far from the sea. These are called continental deserts.

Rain falls on mountains around the Mojave Desert, not in the desert itself.

Rain-shadow deserts

Some deserts, such as the Mojave Desert in the southwest of the United States are known as rain-shadow deserts. When warm, moist air blows against mountains, it rises and becomes cooler. As it cools, the moisture in the air turns into water drops, which form clouds. As the air moves up the mountains, it loses more and more water as rain or snow. By the time the air reaches the other side of the mountains, it is dry and without clouds. There, a rain-shadow desert forms.

At the South Pole in Antarctica, it is too cold to rain.

Coastal deserts

Deserts are found along coasts where the winds are very dry. The Namib in southwest Africa and the Atacama in western South America are both coastal deserts.

Southern Africa's Namib Desert lies beside the cold Atlantic Ocean.

TYPES OF DESERTS

Many people imagine that deserts are made up of huge sand dunes. In fact, only about one-fifth of the world's desert areas are sandy.

Hard rock

The type of desert that forms depends on how much sun, wind, and rain there is, as well as on the type of rock in the ground. Very hard rocks do not break easily, even when the Sun makes them too hot to touch. So the desert is hard and bare.

Uluru, or Ayers Rock, is found in central Australia's desert area. It is Earth's largest rock.

EARTH FACT

The Gobi Desert can be very cold at night. Nowhere else on Earth is it so hot, then so cold, all in just a few hours.

Grains of sand

Softer rocks crack as they warm up
in the Sun and then get cold at night.
They break into small, pebble-size
lumps, then into smaller pieces,
which the wind blows around.
Gradually, they turn into very
tiny pieces of rock—sand grains.

Curved sand dunes
formed by desert
winds are known
as barchan dunes.

Sand dunes

In sandy deserts, the wind blows loose
sand into hills called dunes. These dunes
can take different shapes, such as waves,
curves, or stars, depending on the wind's
direction and speed.

In Australia, desert
rocks and pebbles are
known as gibbers.

DESERT PLANTS

EARTH FACT

When it does rain, the desert suddenly comes alive, as flowers grow quickly and make a carpet of color.

Plants in deserts have a difficult time. They must collect as much water as they can, cope with a scorching Sun, and fight off hungry, plant-eating creatures.

Deep roots

Plants soak up water through their roots. Some desert plants have roots that go down very deep, sometimes 30 feet or more. This is as deep as five people standing on top of each other. Other plants have roots that spread out widely. This helps them take in lots of water quickly when it rains.

The saguaro cactus of southwest North America can grow to be around 50 feet high.

Sturt's desert pea grows in dry areas across much of Australia.

Plant protection

Desert animals eat as many soft plants and leaves as they can find. This is why cacti, acacias, and thornbushes have spines, prickles, or thorns. They protect these plants from being eaten.

Storing water

Some desert plants, such as the cactus, store water in their thick stems. The baobab tree of Africa holds water in its wide trunk.

The baobab tree in Africa can survive severe droughts by storing water in its thick trunk.

ANIMALS OF THE DESERT

The one-humped dromedary camels of Africa and Arabia also live wild in Australia.

Desert animals have to take in water to survive. Yet some of them never drink!

Dry droppings

Many desert animals are able to live just on the water they get from eating fruits and bugs. They do not need to drink extra water. Also, these animals do not lose water from their bodies. They do not **sweat** much, they produce only small amounts of urine (pee), and their droppings are also fairly dry.

Wandering around

Ants and termites are food for many desert creatures, including the spine-covered moloch lizard that lives in deserts in central Australia. Also known as the thorny devil, this creature wanders around slowly, snapping up ants, termites and other insects on its way.

EARTH FACT

Many desert animals have big feet, to stop them from sinking into the sand. Snakes "swim" across the surface of the sand.

The moloch lizard is protected by its sharp spines.

Desert food

Like many desert animals, the fennec fox of the Sahara eats whatever it finds. Its favorite foods are bugs, birds, lizards, and eggs. It will also eat fruits and berries whenever it finds them.

With its huge ears, the fennec fox can hear the noise of bugs running over sand.

THE DESERT AT NIGHT

In the desert, one way to avoid the glaring Sun and scorching heat is to sleep during the day and come out at night.

Listening for danger

During the day, very few animals are seen in the desert. But at night, many creatures are **active**. Most of these have big eyes to see in the dark, even on the blackest nights. Their big ears can hear danger, and their keen noses smell food or predators.

Water holding frogs sleep underground in a slimy bag.

94

When the Sun sets in southern Africa, the bat-eared fox comes out to hunt.

Hunting at night

Most owls hunt at night, so mice and similar desert creatures are always in danger. In North America, the cactus pygmy owl leaves its hole in a saguaro cactus to go hunting. The pharaoh eagle owl that lives in the Sahara and Arabian deserts is so powerful that it can catch and eat other owls!

Burrowing owls live in burrows under the ground in dry areas of North and South America.

Food for the winter

The American desert pocket mouse comes out of its burrow at night to search for seeds and pieces of plants. It takes food back to its burrow to store for the winter.

The American desert pocket mouse hides inside its burrow.

RAIN AND FOREST

Rain forests are well named. They have a lot of tall trees, close together, and it rains and rains and rains!

Warm and wet

Rain forests are wet almost all year round. Tropical rain forests are also very warm. The temperature is at least 68 degrees Fahrenheit on most days.

Rain-forest people get food from plants in the forest.

There are four main layers in a rain forest.

Rain-forest trees grow close together, forming a thick, green covering.

Emergent layer

Canopy layer

Understory layer

Forest floor

Layers of the rain forest

The rain forest has several layers. The floor is a dim and quiet place. Not far above are the tops of tall bushes, shrubs, and young trees. This is the **understory layer**. At the top of the trees is the **canopy layer**. This is a tangle of branches, leaves, flowers, and fruits. It is a busy place, as most rain-forest animals live up there. At the top of the very tallest trees is the **emergent layer**.

Plants and animals

Lots of amazing plants grow fast in a tropical rain forest's damp warmth. Animals of every kind also live there, such as insects, birds, monkeys, and frogs.

TYPES OF RAIN FORESTS

Rain forests grow mainly around the middle of the world, on either side of the equator. This area is called the tropics, and it is warm there all year round.

Warm and cool

Tropical rain forests near the equator are warm all year round. These have the most plants and animals. There are also temperate rain forests in cooler places. These are still very wet. Although cool, they are full of life and have the world's tallest trees, such as the redwoods in the United States and kauri pines in New Zealand. The forest floor is covered with **mosses**, ferns, and creepers.

This gorilla lives in mountain rain forests in central Africa.

NORTH AMERICA

Central America

Amazon

SOUTH AMERICA

Temperate rain forests

Tropical rain forests

Mountain forests

Not all rain forests are on flat lowlands. Some have developed high up on steep hills and mountains and are cooler than tropical rain forests. In the mountain rain forest in southeast China, it is cool and cloudy. There, giant pandas eat bamboo plants.

EARTH FACT

Although rain forests only cover one-sixteenth of Earth's land area, they are home to more than half of all living things.

The blue duiker is a small, shy antelope that lives in the cool rain forests of central and southern Africa.

ASIA

Japan

The biggest rain-forest areas are in South America, Africa, and Southeast Asia.

Philippines

AFRICA

Sumatra

Borneo

Congo

Equator

Madagascar

Java

New Guinea

AUSTRALIA

Tasmania

New Zealand

The goliath tarantula lives on the rain-forest floor in South America and is the world's biggest spider.

RAIN-FOREST ANIMALS

Rain forests are full of creatures, many of which hide away quietly and are difficult to find.

Slimy trails

Rain forests are home to many types of animals. The most common are small insects, such as flies, ants, and termites. Brightly colored butterflies fly between flowers, and snails and slugs leave slimy trails.

Swinging monkeys

The agile spider monkey, which lives in South American rain forests, swings from tree to tree using its hands, feet, and tail to grab and hold on to branches. Below, fish and turtles swim in pools and **swamps**.

The spider monkey has a very long tail

EARTH FACT

The world's biggest snakes live in rain forests. In Africa and Asia, enormous pythons swallow **prey** that is sometimes the size of a pig!

Screeching toucans

Rain forests are also home to cats of all sizes. The marbled cat of Asia looks like a tiny leopard, while the jaguar of South America is almost as big as a lion. In the trees, parrots, macaws, and toucans screech and flap between the branches.

Toucans crack nuts with their huge bills.

The jaguar's spotted coat helps the cat hide in the rain-forest shadows.

DEADLY KILLERS

Rain-forest creatures are always on the lookout for danger. There could be a killer on the next branch!

Deadly poisons

Not all killers are big. Many rain-forest creatures such as spiders and scorpions use poisonous bites or stings to kill their prey. Some tiny South American frogs have deadly poisons in their skin, as well as bright colors to warn other creatures not to eat them! Local people tip their blowdarts, arrows, and spears with this poison.

The poison from one bite of a king cobra can kill an elephant.

EARTH FACT

The poison in the skin of one poison dart frog is so powerful, it could kill up to 20 people!

Tiny poison dart frogs are only as long as your thumb.

Large predators

Some of the most powerful predators live in rain forests. The largest big cat is the tiger, which stalks Asian rain forests for deer and wild pigs. Caimans lurk near swamps in South America and snap up turtles and fish. Growing to about 550 pounds, the same weight as four people, the Amazon's green anaconda is the world's heaviest snake.

Caimans catch fish, turtles, and crabs.

Tigers are the largest hunters in the rain forest.

RAIN-FOREST TREES

Some of the world's tallest, heaviest, and fastest-growing trees are found in rain forests.

Life in a tree

Thousands of creatures depend on rain-forest trees. Caterpillars munch its leaves, hummingbirds sip nectar from its flowers, and monkeys eat its fruits. There are teak trees in Asia, mahogany trees in Africa and Central America, and rosewood trees around the world. The kapok tree of Central and South America grows to be 230 feet tall—as high as an 18-story building.

Rosewood trees are under threat from loggers, who cut them for their sweet-smelling wood.

Emerald tree boas wrap themselves around branches and wait for prey.

104

Using camouflage

Some animals depend so much on trees, that they look like them! Stick insects, or "walking sticks," resemble twigs. Leaf insects and the tree boa snake are green, just like leaves. The colorful flower mantis is disguised as a flower. Looking like part of the surroundings in order to avoid being seen is called **camouflage**.

Insects fall into a pitcher plant and are digested

Cooktown orchids grow in rain forests in northeastern Australia.

THE FLOOR AND CANOPY

Both the floor and the canopy of the rain forest are full of amazing creatures.

The forest floor

Some of the world's most exciting animals slip through the shadows of the forest floor. In West Africa, forest elephants and lowland gorillas live there. In South American and Asian rain forests, tapirs feed on the plants of the forest floor. This level gets little light because of the thick canopy above. When a huge tree falls, sunlight can break through. New plants can then grow.

EARTH FACT

The rafflesia of Southeast Asia is the world's largest flower, at 3 feet wide.

The sloth hangs from branches by its long, curved claws.

The rafflesia attracts flies to carry its pollen by smelling like rotten meat!

Pygmy marmosets eat the sap of rain-forest trees. They are the size of a human fist.

The canopy

The canopy is teeming with animals, which eat the plants all round. Colorful birds such as honeyeaters and motmots fly among the branches. Eagles prey on monkeys, sloths, snakes, and birds. Some animals in the canopy never come down to the ground. These include monkeys and lizards, such as iguanas and geckos.

The tapir is a piglike animal. Its fleshy nose helps it grab tasty leaves.

107

DISAPPEARING RAIN FORESTS

Rain forests are the richest places in the world for wildlife. But they are also places that are the most at risk, and they are disappearing fast.

Once the forest has been cleared, the land is used to grow crops.

Laws against illegal logging are often ignored

Destroying trees

Rain forests face many dangers, especially in the tropics. There, trees are cut down for their strong timber, which is known as hardwood. Without trees, many forest animals have no homes and with no tree roots, forest soil gets washed away by heavy rain and blocks nearby rivers.

Cleared for crops

Rain forests are being cleared by fire in order to grow farm crops, such as sugarcane and oil palm trees. Many areas are also being planted with grass to feed cows and other **livestock**. Some rain forest animals are in danger because they are hunted for their meat.

Saving rain forests

All kinds of rain-forest animals, from butterflies and beetles to tigers, gorillas, and rhinos, are at great risk. We must work hard to save rain forests, with their wonderful plants and amazing creatures.

Orangutans may be extinct in 30 years.

109

TOP AND BOTTOM

At the top of the world is the North Pole, and at the bottom is the South Pole. These places are cold even in the summer and very, very cold in the winter.

Summer and winter

On Earth, the farthest points in the north and south are called the poles. The Arctic is in the far north, around the North Pole, and the Antarctic is in the far south, around the South Pole. These areas are very cold and are mainly covered in ice. Even though the Sun never sets in the summer, it remains cold because the Sun's rays are weak and low in the sky. In the winter, the Sun never rises and it is freezing cold.

North Pole

South Pole

Earth's poles lie at opposite ends of the world and appear icy-white when seen from space.

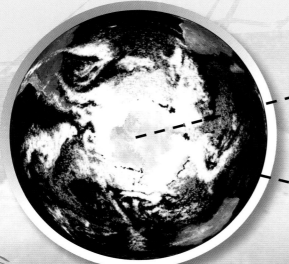

Life in the cold

Even in these harsh places, there is still life. Fish, seals, penguins, and whales swim in the seas. Small plants, such as mosses and herbs, grow in the Arctic. People live there, too.

Traditionally, Inuit people of the far north catch fish through ice holes.

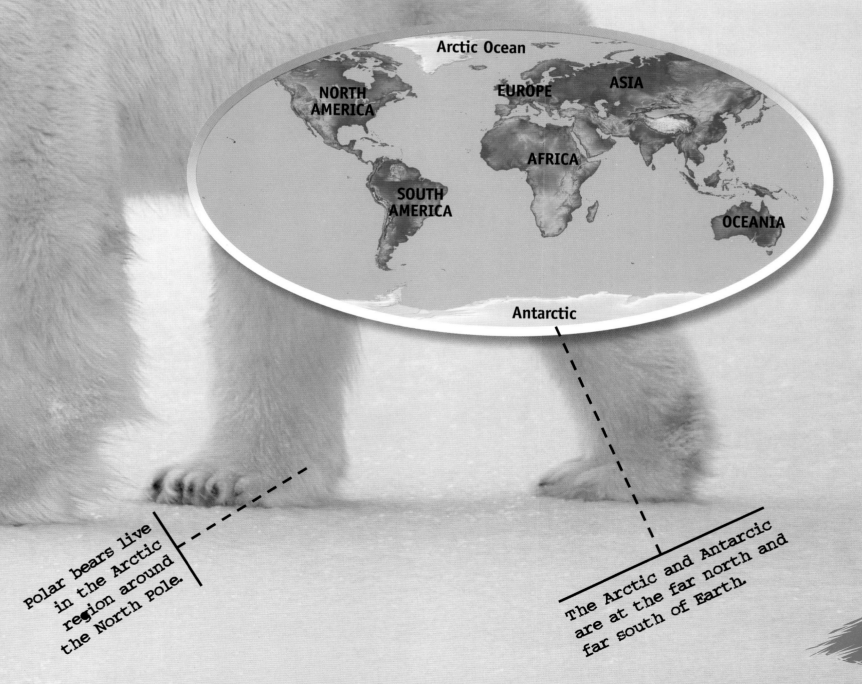

Polar bears live in the Arctic region around the North Pole.

The Arctic and Antarcic are at the far north and far south of Earth.

THE ARCTIC— FROZEN OCEAN

There is no land in the North Pole or for hundreds of miles around it. Much of the Arctic is a cold, shallow ocean. This is covered with ice during the long winter. Some of this ice melts in the summer.

Smallest ocean

The Arctic is the world's smallest ocean. Its average depth is only 3,280 feet. In the winter, more than half of it is covered by a vast, floating sheet of ice, 7 to 10 feet thick. In the summer, some of the ice melts, forming blocks called ice floes.

EARTH FACT

The largest known polar bear stood more than 10 feet tall.

A mother polar bear teaches her young how to hunt.

North America — **Asia** — **North Pole** — **Greenland**

North America — **Asia** — **North Pole** — **Greenland**

The Arctic ice sheet is twice as large in the winter as it is in the summer.

■ Winter ice extent   ■ Summer ice extent

Arctic animals

Along the Arctic shores there is plenty of food, including fish and shellfish. These are eaten by large hunters, such as seals and walrus. The biggest predator is the polar bear. It eats seals and even small whales. When it cannot find animals to eat, the polar bear will eat plants.

Walrus spend most of the year in the Arctic.

In the summer, the Arctic ice cracks into floating ice floes.

TUNDRA AND FORESTS

Beyond the Arctic ice lie the tundra lands. It is too cold for trees to grow there. South of the tundra, about 1,550 miles from the North Pole, are the vast forests of North America, Europe, and Asia.

Treeless tundra

The tundra is covered in snow during the winter. Only small plants can grow there, such as mosses and small shrubs. In the short summer, animals such as lemmings, arctic foxes, and musk oxen feed on them. Caribou also arrive from farther south, to feed on the plants.

Arctic poppies bloom in the tundra in the summer.

EARTH FACT

Birds and sea animals travel to the Arctic to eat the plants that grow there in the summer.

Northern forests

The forests of the far north are called boreal forests, or taiga. Their trees are mainly **conifers**, such as pines, firs, and larches. They are **evergreen**, with leaves all year round. Animals such as elk, wolves, bears, and grouse live there.

Northern forests are covered in snow in the winter.

The gray wolf has a thick coat to keep it warm in the forest.

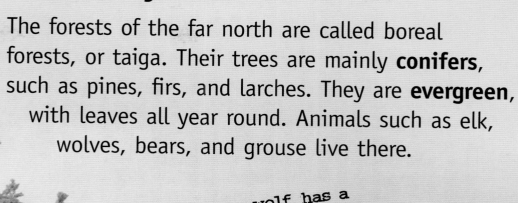

The Sami people of northern Finland follow caribou when they migrate north to the tundra in the summer.

THE ANTARCTIC— FROZEN LAND

Antarctica is at the opposite end of the world to the Arctic. It is a frozen land surrounded by an ocean and is the coldest place on Earth. The average temperature is 32 degrees Fahrenheit.

Hidden mountains

Antarctica is a vast **landmass** covered by a giant ice cap, which is an average of 6,560 feet thick, although in some places it is 14,765 feet thick. Under the ice are mountains, valleys and lakes. In summer, some plants grow when the ice melts.

Antarctica's coast has steep cliffs and icy seas.

Emperor penguins huddle together to protect their chicks and keep them warm.

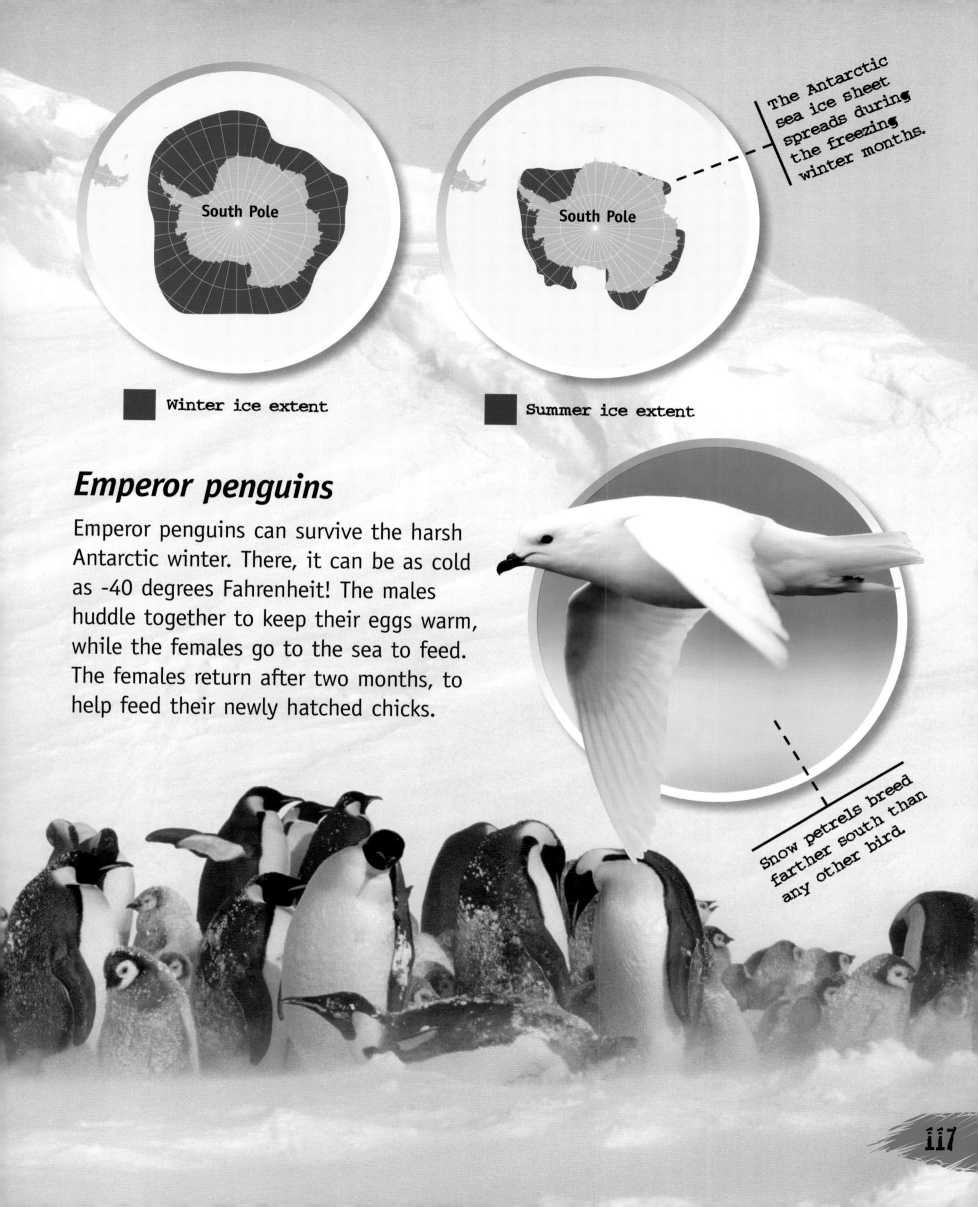

South Pole

South Pole

The Antarctic sea ice sheet spreads during the freezing winter months.

■ Winter ice extent

■ Summer ice extent

Emperor penguins

Emperor penguins can survive the harsh Antarctic winter. There, it can be as cold as -40 degrees Fahrenheit! The males huddle together to keep their eggs warm, while the females go to the sea to feed. The females return after two months, to help feed their newly hatched chicks.

Snow petrels breed farther south than any other bird

SOUTHERN OCEAN

Around Antarctica is the great Southern Ocean. It is one and a half times bigger and much deeper than the Arctic Ocean. It teems with life during the summer months.

Food chain

The Southern Ocean, like the Arctic Ocean, is cold but rich in **nutrients**. During the summer months, when there is plenty of light, tiny **phytoplankton** grow. These are eaten by tiny **zooplankton**, which are in turn food for bigger creatures, such as fish and squid.

The Antarctic fin whale is 72 feet long.

Giant shoals of krill

One of the most important creatures in the Southern Ocean is the tiny krill, a cousin of the shrimp. Millions of krill come together to form giant **shoals**. They are eaten by all kinds of Antarctic animals, including seals, penguins, and seabirds. Great whales, such as the blue and humpback whale, also feast on krill.

Antarctic krill that are not eaten can live for up to six years.

Antarctic fish have natural chemical "antifreeze" in their blood.

ISLANDS OF ICE

Icebergs are massive lumps of ice that have broken off ice caps around polar lands. Antarctica has the biggest icebergs. Some are the size of small countries.

Layers of ice

Over time, snow that falls on polar lands is squashed into layers of ice. These layers are squeezed, until they slide off sideways toward the coast. At the coast, big lumps of ice break off into the ocean and drift away as icebergs.

Chinstrap penguins sometimes breed on icebergs.

Only one-eighth of an iceberg is above water.

Resting and hiding

Icebergs are like floating islands. They are ideal resting places for seabirds, such as petrels and penguins, as well as for seals. Icebergs also contain handy hiding places. The leopard seal lurks around the edges of icebergs, waiting to grab a penguin or small seal as it passes by.

The leopard seal has sharp front teeth for feeding on prey.

PROTECT THE POLES

Even though polar regions are far away, they are at risk from the effects of the modern world.

Mining for minerals

About 300 years ago, people began sailing to polar seas to kill seals, whales, and other animals. People also explored the land for valuable minerals, such as oil, coal, and precious gems. Today, oil wells and mines dot the land and oil spills from huge tanker ships have ruined some areas.

A gray whale is covered in oil following an oil spill in Alaska.

Damage caused by oil spills can last for many years.

There are many oil pipelines and tankers in Alaska.

Melting ice

Polar lands and seas need protection from pollution. Dangerous chemicals are spreading in polar waters, and the protective **ozone gas** high in the sky has been damaged by chemicals from aerosol spray cans and refridgerators. Many scientists believe that global warming is melting the polar ice caps, destroying the natural **habitats** of people and animals.

WET WORLD

Only 30 percent of Earth's surface is made up of dirt and rocks. The other 70 percent consists of water in rivers, lakes, seas, and oceans.

Marlin are among the largest, fastest fish in the world's oceans.

Salty water

Most of the world's water is the salty water of the seas and oceans. This includes warm, shallow **bays** and colorful, tropical **reefs**, as well as the huge, wide-open expanses and cold, dark depths of the oceans.

124

Arctic Ocean

Atlantic
Ocean

Mediterranean
Sea

Caribbean
Sea

Equator

Pacific
Ocean

Indian
Ocean

Southern Ocean

Earth has seven oceans.

Mysterious oceans

Oceans are the largest areas of salty water. Seas, such as the Caribbean and Mediterranean, are smaller and partially surrounded by land. The oceans are so vast that there is still plenty of exploring to do. Many mysteries lurk in their depths!

Tropical islands are surrounded by a vast ocean.

On a rescue mission, the coast guard often has to battle stormy seas.

MEET THE SEA

Without rivers, seas, and oceans around, the world would dry up. Luckily, rivers pour water into them and keep them topped up.

In the summer, flowers bloom on salt marshes.

Pelicans feed on the fish that swim in estuary waters.

Sand and mud

As rivers get close to the sea, they widen into a mouth called an **estuary**, or bay. Rivers carry tiny pieces of sand and mud. Close to the sea, rivers slow down and the sand and mud fall to the bottom. This is why estuaries and bays often have shallow mudflats, salt marshes, and sandbanks.

A saltwater crocodile warms up on a mudbank before sliding into the water.

Fiddler crabs live in salt marshes.

Teeming with life

Although the surface of the mud and sand may look bare, underneath it is teeming with life. There, creatures, such as worms, shrimps, crabs, and shellfish, live in huge numbers. As the tide comes in, these animals come out to feed on tiny pieces of food. But when they do this, they are in danger from hungry fish and birds.

BEACHES AND ROCKY SHORES

The sea washes in sand and pebbles on the beach and washes up seaweed and sea animals. Where the ocean crashes against rocks, they form tall cliffs and rock pools below.

Waves can wear rocks into amazing shapes, such as these tall stacks.

Sandy beaches

Sand is made of tiny pieces of broken rock and animal shells that have been broken up by the movement of the sea in currents. Some animals spend part of their lives in the sand, such as sea turtles.

Sea lions crowd onto beaches to rest.

Cliffs and rock pools

Many animals live on the cliffs created by the waves. Birds such as gannets nest on the tiny ledges. They fly out to sea to catch fish for their chicks. As the tide goes out, it leaves small pools in the rocks. These teem with life, including crabs and small fish. Anemones in the pools sting tiny creatures with their tentacles.

Cliff-nesting birds are safe from many enemies.

Anemones look like flowers, but most are poisonous.

SHALLOWS AND CORAL REEFS

Most sea creatures live in the shallow sea less than 660 feet deep, around the coast. Coral reefs have more kinds of wildlife than any other place in the sea.

In the shallows

Plants grow in shallow waters, where there is plenty of sunlight. The plants can also feed on nutrients that are deposited by rivers.

Few places are as colorful as a coral reef.

Manatees live in shallow and warm bays, estuaries, and lagoons.

Seaweeds, such as bladderwrack and hollow green-weed, form beautiful underwater gardens.

Coral reefs

Coral reefs grow in warm water. Tiny coral animals build stony cups around themselves for protection, and when they die they leave behind these hard cups. These cups build up into the reef. Different kinds of corals make different shapes, such as vases, horns, and fans. Brightly colored fish swim in the reef and predators, such as the black-tipped reef shark, prowl around the edge waiting to snap up prey.

Giant groupers are predators that can swallow other reef fish whole.

THE OPEN OCEAN

In the open ocean, there is nowhere to hide. Animals that live there have to cope with big waves, the hot Sun, and predators of all kinds.

EARTH FACT

The largest fish is the whale shark. It is as big as a school bus but is not dangerous.

Killer whales hunt many creatures, including seals, fish, and seabirds.

Biggest fish

The whale shark swims along with its huge mouth wide open. As it swims, it takes in large amounts of water. The water contains tiny plants and animals called phytoplankton and zooplankton, which are eaten by the enormous shark.

Whale sharks swim very slowly through the water as they feed.

The oceans contain billions of tiny creatures, such as the copepod.

Plant plankton

There are few seaweeds in the open ocean, but there are billions of very tiny plants called phytoplankton. These are eaten by very small animals, which are then food for small fish, squid, and other creatures. Larger fish eat these, and are in turn food for bigger creatures, right up to the largest ocean hunters, such as the great white shark and killer whale.

THE DEEP OCEAN

Far below the ocean's surface is a dim and gloomy world. In the deepest parts of the ocean, there is no day or night and no winter or summer. It is dark and cold all the time.

Strange creatures

As the ocean becomes deeper, there is less sunlight, so plants cannot grow. Some amazing creatures live there, such as jellyfish, worms, squid, and octopuses. They eat dead creatures that drift down from above or hunt and eat each other. Some of them even glow in the dark! They have special body parts that make light. This is called **bioluminescence**.

In the deepest sea, the anglerfish uses a glowing light to attract fish.

134

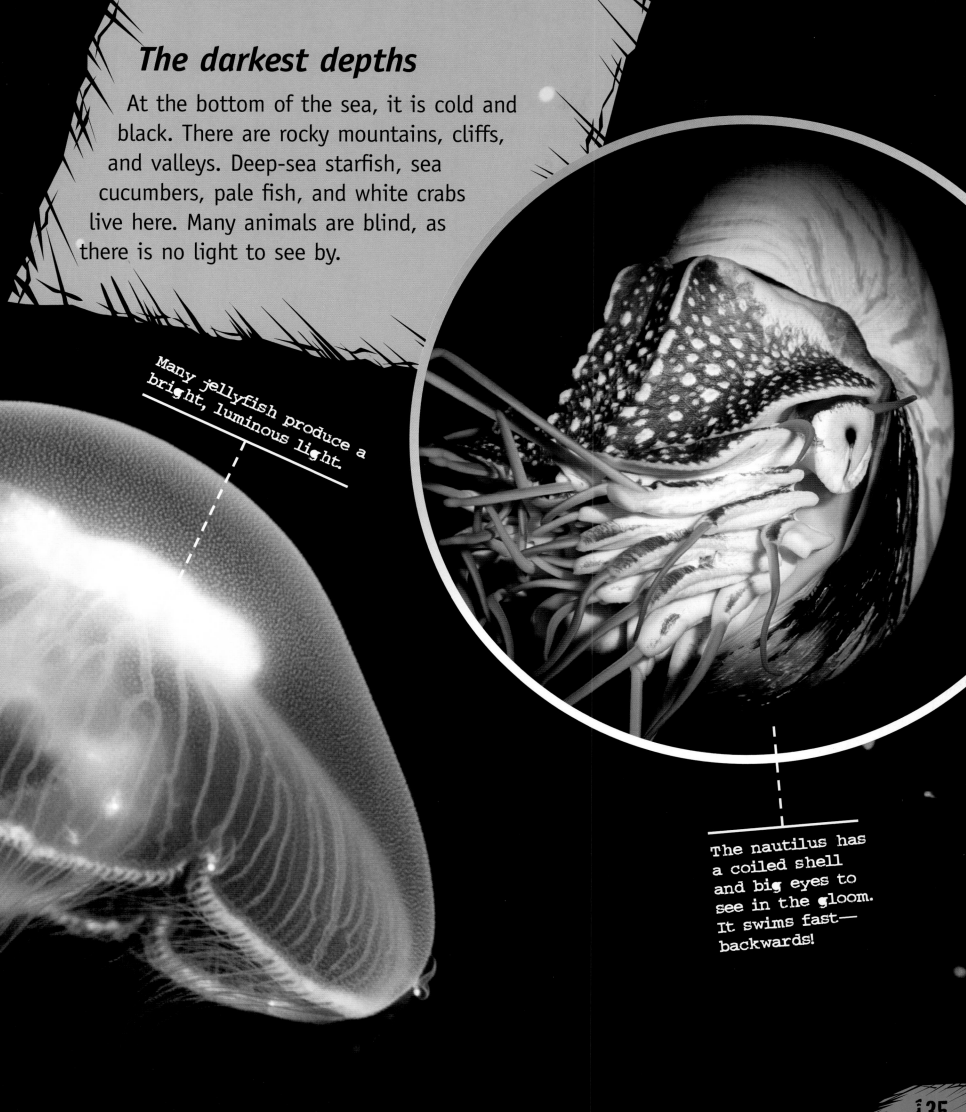

The darkest depths

At the bottom of the sea, it is cold and black. There are rocky mountains, cliffs, and valleys. Deep-sea starfish, sea cucumbers, pale fish, and white crabs live here. Many animals are blind, as there is no light to see by.

Many jellyfish produce a bright, luminous light.

The nautilus has a coiled shell and big eyes to see in the gloom. It swims fast—backwards!

SEAS AND OCEANS AT RISK

Oceans and seas are in trouble. We throw garbage into them, pollute them with chemicals, and catch too much of their wildlife.

EARTH FACT

There are more than 170,000 species of animals in the ocean.

Plastic bags kill sea turtles, who mistake them for jellyfish.

Birds affected by oil spills cannot fly or catch food.

Damaged by pollution

Seas and oceans are becoming more and more polluted. People litter the beach and dump garbage overboard from ships and boats. Pipes from factories pour dangerous chemicals into the water. A giant oil tanker may have an accident and spill its thick, black oil. This floats on the sea and kills fish, seabirds, and other wildlife.

Litter left or washed up on a beach can harm wildlife.

Flooding lowlands

The problem of global warming will greatly affect seas and oceans all around the world. This warming may cause water to expand and the ice at the poles to melt. This could raise ocean levels and flood low-lying areas of land, making millions of people homeless.

Cities such as Venice, Italy are at great risk of coastal flooding.

GLOSSARY

Active
Moving, not asleep.

Altitude
A place's height above
sea level.

Arid
Extremely dry, with
very little rain or other
forms of moisture.

Atmosphere
The layer of gases
around Earth.

Bay
Part of a coast that curves
around an area of sea.

Bioluminescence
When living things
produce light by special
chemical processes.

Camouflage
Colors and patterns
that blend in with the
surroundings, making a
creature difficult to see.

Canopy layer
The main level of
branches, leaves, and
flowers in a rain forest,
high above the
ground.

Climate
Earth's weather
patterns and its
temperature.

Comet
Big ball of ice
and dust going
around the Sun.

Conifers
Trees that produce their
seeds in cones.

Continent
A large landmass, such as
Africa and Australia.

Crops
Plants grown by people
for food or products.

Crust
Hard, rocky outermost
layer of Earth.

Current
Flowing movements
in water.

Delta
Area of flat land near the
coast where a river splits
into many channels.

Dissolved
Tiny particles spread out
in a liquid.

Emergent layer
The tallest trees in
a forest, above the
main canopy layer.

Environment
The surroundings, including rocks, soil, plants, animals, and the weather.

Epicenter
Place on Earth's surface above the center of an earthquake, where it is felt most strongly.

Equator
An imaginary line around the middle of the planet, midway between the North Pole and South Pole.

Erosion
The wearing away of soil and rocks by rain, wind, the Sun, sand, and ice.

Eruption
When liquid rock from deep in Earth comes up through the crust.

Estuary
The end, or mouth, of a river, where it widens and flows into the sea.

Evergreen
Trees that have some leaves throughout the year.

Expansion
Getting bigger when heated or frozen.

Fjord
Deep-sea inlet created by a glacier.

Floodplain
Area of land by a river that is regularly flooded.

Fossil
Remains of a living thing preserved in rocks.

Geyser
Spring that erupts hot water and steam, caused by a magma pool close to the surface.

Glacier
Huge river of ice sliding downhill.

Global warming
Heating up of Earth caused by changes in the gases that make up its atmosphere.

Gorge
Deep valley cut by a river.

Gravity
The force that pulls objects toward the ground.

Habitats
Types of places where animals and plants live, such as a forest, lake, or seashore.

Hibernate
Sleep through the winter when food is difficult to find.

Hurricane
A violent tropical storm.

Ice age
Period of time when Earth was much colder, and large areas were covered with ice.

Igneous rock
Rock formed when melted lava or magma cools and hardens.

Insulate
Prevent heat or cold from being lost.

Landmass
A large, continuous area of land.

Lava
When magma erupts from a volcano, it is known as lava.

GLOSSARY

Livestock
Animals kept by people, especially on farms, such as cows, sheep, and pigs.

Magma
Hot, semiliquid rock that makes up Earth's outer core.

Mantle
A layer between Earth's crust and its core.

Metamorphic rock
Rock that is changed by great heat and pressure, but without melting.

Migrate
To make a long journey each year, and then to return again.

Minerals
A large range of natural substances that make up rocks and soil.

Mosses
Soft, spongy plants that grow in very wet places.

Nutrients
Substances used as food by living things.

Oxygen
A gas that is in the air we breathe. Oxygen is also found in water and is used by underwater creatures to breathe.

Ozone gas
A form of oxygen that is high in the sky and helps protect against some of the Sun's harmful rays.

Phytoplankton
Tiny plants, mostly too small to see, that float in seas, oceans, and large lakes.

Plain
Flat area, usually covered by grass or similar low plants.

Polar regions
Very cold areas around the North and South poles.

Predator
An animal that hunts others for food.

Pressure
A pressing or pushing force.

Prey
An animal that is hunted for food.

Reef
A large, rocky part of the seabed, usually built by tiny coral animals.

Sediment
Tiny pieces or particles that settle into layers.

Sedimentary rock
Rock formed by squeezing together particles of sediments.

Shoal
A large gathering of water animals, such as fish or krill.

Silt
Very small or fine particles of sediments, like slippery mud.

Sinkhole
Deep hole at the surface into which water flows underground.

Sound waves
Vibrations that carry sound.

Supernova
A massive exploding star.

Swamp
Place with both ground and water, often with lots of muddy pools and soft, wet soil.

Sweat
To give off moisture, perspiration, through the pores of the skin.

Tectonic plate
A large, curved section of Earth's outer crust that floats on the molten rock beneath it.

Temperate
Places where it is neither very hot nor very cold, usually with warm summers and cool winters.

Tornado
A spinning column of air that causes destruction.

Trace
A sign, or tiny remains of an animal or plant that died long ago.

Transform fault
Area where one tectonic plate slides past another.

Tropics
The region around the middle of the planet where it is very warm all year.

Tsunami
Massive, powerful wave set off by an earthquake, volcano, or landslip.

Understory layer
Bushes, shrubs, young trees, and other low-growing plants in a forest.

Volcanic plug
Central part of a volcano, where the lava has turned very hard.

Water vapor
Water in the form of an invisible gas that floats in air.

Wetland
Place with large amounts of water, such as a river, lake, marsh, or swamp.

Wind turbine
Tall tower with spinning blades that makes electricity from wind energy.

Zooplankton
Tiny animals, mostly too small to see, that float in seas, oceans, and large lakes.

INDEX

Sandy Creek
NEW YORK

An Imprint of Sterling Publishing
387 Park Avenue South
New York, NY 10016

SANDY CREEK and the distinctive Sandy Creek logo are registered trademarks of Barnes & Noble, Inc.

Copyright © QEB Publishing, Inc. 2012

This 2012 custom edition published exclusively for Sandy Creek by QEB Publishing, Inc.

Design and Editorial: Calcium

ISBN: 978-1-4351-4406-4 (print format)

A CIP record for this book is available from the Library of Congress.

For information about custom editions, special sales, and premium and corporate purchases, please contact Sterling Special Sales at 800-805-5489 or specialsales@sterlingpublishing.com.

Manufactured in China
Lot #:
2   4   6   8   10   9   7   5   3   1
09/12

Picture credits

Key: t = top, b = bottom, c = center, l = left, r = right

Corbis 3t STR-epa, 9t Colin Garratt/Milepost 921/2, 10–11 Julie Dermansky, 34b Bryn Colton, 34–35 Nic Bothma/epa/Assignments Photographers, 42–43 Guenter Rossenbach, 46–47 Diego Azubel/epa, 60–61 Michael S. Yamashita, 61t Bettmann, 62–63 Anatoly Maltsev/epa, 63t Menno Boermans-Aurora Photos, 64–65 Jeremy Horner, 65t STR/epa, 72b Mike Hollingshead/Science Faction, 72–73 George Steinmetz, 73t Chris Mattison, 76–77 Visuals Unlimited, 116–117 Tim Davis, 123t Reuters, 123b Karen Kasmauski, 136–137 Reuters

Getty Images 24b Joseph Van Os, 26c Stephen Alvarez, 30–31 Kreg Holt, 31t Phillippe Bourseiller, 33t National Geographic, 38 Kim Westerskov, 41b Time & Life Pictures, 44–45t Panoramic Images, 45b, 52b Paul Chesley, 53t Dario Mitidieri-Contributor, 55t, 56–57 Arctic-Images, 57b Travel Pix, 68–69, 78–79 STasker, 85t Chris Sattlberger, 86–87 Jeff Foott, 89t Peter Pearson, 89b Paul Chesley, 90–91 Lee Frost, 96b Maria Stenzel, 101t Pete Oxford, 102–103 Norbert Wu, 105b DEA/R. Sacco, 112–113 Daniel J Cox, 115b Jorn Georg Tomter, 118–119 Tui De

Roy, 119t Flip Nicklin, 119b Bill Curtsinger, 122–123 Natalie Fobes/Science Faction, 131b Norbert Wu, 134b Peter David

Louise Downey 11t, 69t, 71b

Michael Penn 33b NYT / Redux / eyevine

NASA 2–3 GSFC/Jacques Descloitres/MODIS Rapid Response Team, 4–5 ESA/STScI/JHU/K. Kuntz, 4c ESA/J. Hester/A. Loll (ASU), 7b

Nature Picture Library 95b John Cancalosi

NHPA 14–15 Photoshot, 15b Woodfall Wild Images, 16–17 World Pictures, 20–21 Tom & Therisa Stack, 21b Xinhua, 43t, 58–59 VWPics, 94–95 Martin Harvey, 94b ANT Photo Library, 99t Nigel J Dennis, 104–105 John Shaw, 107b Martin Harvey, 108–109 Martin Wendler, 108l Martin Harvey, 111t, 121t, Bryan & Cherry Alexander, 124l A N T Photo Library, 126b Nigel J Dennis, 131t Trevor McDonald, 132–133 Gerard Lacz, 135r Kevin Schafer

Photolibrary 117t David B Fleetham, 120–121 Kevin Schafer

Science Photo Library 7t Mark Garlick, 8b SPL, 9b Lynette Cook, 10b Karim Agabi, 14c Gary Hincks, 16b Gary Hinks, 18c Javier Trueba/MSF, 27t Daniel Sambraus, 39t W. Haxby/Lamont-Doherty Earth observatory, 40b Jacques Jangoux, 50–51 Gary Hincks, 51b Gary Hincks, 59b Dr Ken MacDonald, 60b Gary Hincks, 64b Gary Hincks, 73b Gary Hincks, 75r Lino Pastorelli, 77t Gary Hincks, 78b Gary Hincks

Shutterstock 2c Donald Gargano, 3b Beboy, 5b Linda Brotkorb, 6–7 sdecoret, 8–9 Galyna Andrushko, 12–13 Nikki Bidgood, 13t Vulkanette, 13b Jose Gil, 15t Beschi,17r Elena Elisseeva, 18–19 Dmitri Melnik, 18b Don Bendickson, 19b Jiri Vaclavek, 21t Geowulf, 22–23 szefei, 23b nikolpetr, 23t, 24–25 K. Kolygo, 25t George Burba, 25b Roger De Marfa, 26–27 Sally Scott, 28t Boykov, 28–29 Imagine Images Alastair Pidgen, 29b Xavier Marchant, 29t Pavelk, 30b Sam D Cruz, 32–33 marchello, 32b mountainpix, 35t Gertjan Hooijer, 35b Atlaspix, 36–37 federicofoto, 37t bierchen, 39b Donald Gargano, 40–41 Elisabeth Holm, 41t Perkoptimal, 42b Michael Shake, 43b Vinicius Tupinamba, 44b Martin D. Vonka, 45t Thor Jorgen Udvang, 46bl agophoto, 46br steve estvanik, 47br Eric Gevaert, 48–49 Jon Naustdalslid, 48b Beboy, 49t Lysithee, 52–53 Supertrooper, 54–55 Volodymyr Goinyk, 54b iNNOCENt, 55b Caitlin Mirra, 57t Gian Corrêa Saléro, 59t Supertrooper, 62b Juha Sompinmäki, 66–67 Scott Prokop, 66b Paolo Albertosi, 67t WORAKIT, 69b Dark O, 70t Basel101658, 70c majeczka, 70b Jozsef Szasz-Fabian, 70–71 Paul Aniszewski, 74–75 James "BO" Insogna, 76b Ramon Berk, 79t Wonlopcolors, 79b Sakis Papadopoulos, 80–81 T.W. van Urk, 81r I. Quintanilla, 82c Louise Cukrov, 82–83 Amir Hossein Biparva, 83t Alexey Goosev, 83b Vova Pomortzeff, 84–85 Stasys Eidiejus, 87t Ke Wang, 87b Angel's Gate Inc, 88–89 Kaspars Grinvalds, 90b Jo Ann Snover, 91t Ashley Whitworth, 92–93 Dmytro Korolov, 93t Steve Lovegrove, 93b Hagit Berkovich, 95c David Nagy, 96–97 Antonio Jorge Nunes, 98b Donald Gargano, 99b Olga Shelego, 100–101 Jamie Robinson, 101b Leo, 102b Luis Louro, 103t Timothy Craig Lubcke, 104b Sergey I, 105t chai kian shin, 106–107 Alvaro Pantoja, 106b Vova Pomortzeff, 107t Karel Gallas, 109b Simone van den Berg, 110b Stasys Eidiejus, 110–111 Jan Martin Will, 113b Armin Rose, 113t, 114b Gail Johnson, 114–115 TTphoto, 115t James R Hearn, 116t Vera Bogaerts, 117c Rich Lindie, 121b Jan Martin Will, 124–125 Chen Z, 125b Eric Gevaert, 125t Khlobystov Alexey, 126–127 David Mail, 127t Susan flashman, 127b Marco Alegria, 128–129 Stuart Elflett, 128b Pichugin Dmitry, 129t Jerome Whittingham, 129r Holger W, 130–131 Elisei Shafer, 130b Doug Perrine, 133t James Watt, 133b Roland Birke, 134–135 Kevin Schafer, 136l Jon Milnes, 137t Juha Sompinmäki, 137b Verdelho, 138b Leo, 141t Jo Ann Snover